To: B·

Best wish

Richard Allen Lium

Theo-Economics®

Roland J. Hill, D. Min.

Helping Hands Press
P.O. Box 133
Keene, TX 76059

Edited by Ken McFarland
Cover design by Hallerin Hill, Raymond Wade

ISBN: 0-9639357-0-4

Dedication

To my wife — Susie M. Hill

Contents

Acknowledgments

No book is the work of one person, and this book is no exception. I am deeply indebted to many people who have in one way or another assisted in bringing this book to you.

Special thanks go to Dr. and Mrs. Franklin S. Hill, Sr., my parents, for the sacrifices made to provide for me the kind of spiritual, mental, and educational foundation that has allowed me to be a free spirit and independent thinker.

Thanks also to . . .

My brothers — pastors Byron Hill and Franklin Hill III — for special support, friendship, and encouragement. To my brother Mr. Hallerin Hill for his help on cover design and public relations. To my sister and brother-in-law, Dr. and Mrs. Michael Harris, for their feedback on the concepts presented in the book and for their encouragement. To Elder Henry Billingslea for his giant push that propelled me to write. To Mr. Tim Jacobsen for guidance in the project. To Dr. Marvin Anderson, my boss, for encouraging the entrepreneurial spirit in me. To Mr. Ken McFarland and Miss Tricia Schnell for editorial work.

Finally, a very special thanks to Mrs. Susie M. Hill, my wife, who has listened to my research for over eighteen years and encouraged me to share it with others. Thanks as well to Mian and Sonia for being wonderful children.

All praise and thanks go to God, who has taken just an ordinary person to use as a vessel through which truth is shared with others.

Introduction

Prophets of prosperity on one hand and doomsday reporters on the other — who can we believe about the economy?

After searching for nearly two decades, I could find no real answers to America's economic dilemma in today's economic theories. Answers given by economists to our predicament sounded profound but on closer inspection left much to be desired. What you and I need now are sound fiscal policies designed to turn around an out-of-control economy.

Theo-Economics is about an economy that includes all people. It is about an economy that works. It is about God's economy — an economy that operates above and yet through all human economies.

In this book, you will discover new, in-depth ways of looking at the economy. Your thinking will be challenged by the biblical truths presented in the following pages. I personally have been challenged and changed by the concepts presented here — by the insights into this new economy. Theo-Economics is so different that it might be considered radical.

Please don't let the word *economy* frighten you. I have written this book to be understandable by everyone. I do suggest, though, that you read it through several times. I have discovered that the more you read the principles in Theo-Economics, the more real and exciting they become. God's blessings be on all those who read and apply the principles outlined here.

Roland J. Hill, D. Min.
Keene, Texas

1

The Purpose of an Economy

We humans cannot live without some type of economy. Economy is a vital part of our lives. In this chapter you will discover the need for an economy to exist. You will find that you are an economist in your own right. This chapter is about empowering you — about challenging you to consider and assume your place in the economy of which you are a part.

Nearly six billion people live on Planet Earth. Of that six billion, 248 million live in the United States of America. And of that 248 million in the United States, about 90 percent live in metropolitan areas. With the migration of Americans away from farms to the cities came the need for people to work together to provide more to meet life's basic material needs.

On the farm, food was grown, cows were milked, butter was churned, clothes were made, and meat was eaten from one's own livestock. An economy was needed, but only a small and simple economy that would supply the few things that couldn't be supplied on the farm.

So it was with our nation in its early days. It was a simple life. Ninety percent of the people lived on farms. They were able to provide most of their needs themselves. But after two hundred years of unprecedented growth, our nation's economy — like our needs — has grown more complicated. But complexity doesn't necessarily mean effectiveness or soundness. In many cases it simply hides ignorance and inefficiency. Our country (and you and I are the country) needs, more than ever, a simpler and sounder economy. But simpler does not mean simplistic — looking at complex issues and denying intricate dimensions. Rather, it means taking complex issues and making them understandable and workable.

What fascinates me is how our nation and some of its leaders have led us to believe that if something sounds difficult, it must be solid. In fact, the more difficult it sounds (technical terms, big words, obscure theories), the more we think it is profound and thus correct. Look at business textbooks. Listen to the speeches of politicians. Eavesdrop on people's conversations. Notice how they all seek to impress with big words and high-sounding theories. It's really a game Americans have learned to play. So is the game played in economics. Big words, complex mathematical formulas, deep-sounding theories — all to make a relatively simple subject difficult.

The purpose of an economy is to provide an organized way of producing and distributing material supplies to meet the needs of people in the most useful and honest way possible. It doesn't take super intelligence to do that. The history of our nation bears this out. It wasn't the eggheads who started businesses in this country. They were too busy writing about what they believed needed to be done instead of getting up and making things happen. The so-called superbrains have spent their time telling us what couldn't be done. They are experts in telling us how bad things are. But where are the answers?

What I have come to understand is that economics is the work of everyone. It is not just the work of a few big-name university graduates. From the janitor to the chief executive officer in a Fortune 500 company, all must be involved in economics.

R.C. Sproul, Jr., in his book *Money Matters*, writes, "An educated layman is more effective than ten economic scholars."[1]

This was not intended to put down professional economists, but it does make the point that everyone is an economist. We all can and must take part in meeting each other's needs. We all must be producers and not just consumers. A healthy economy is based on the idea that everyone is important—that everyone is intelligent, that everyone can and ought to be allowed to enter into the economic discussion. I believe that even the most simple-minded person can contribute something to the economy.

I was leading a very difficult group of people some years ago. They were critical, uncooperative, and sometimes just plain mean. I really didn't know how to deal with them. There was one man in the group to whom I was drawn. Everyone thought he was a basket case, and to be honest, he was. If you were to talk to him, his present and past blended together. Sometimes you wouldn't know if he was talking about 1940 or 1980. But he had some deep insights into people. He gave me some sound advice on dealing with this cantankerous group—and his advice worked. Was he a leader? No! Did he help a leader? Yes!

Any talk about economics takes for granted the idea that people need each other. The fact is that no man is an island. Jesus made this point when He instructed us that we should love our neighbor as ourselves. We love our neighbor not just because it is morally right. We love our neighbor because we need him. The poet Kipling says it in these words:

> For the strength of the pack is the wolf,
> And the strength of the wolf is the pack.

Being an individual is important. But an individual is of little importance without the group. The scientist, of himself, is of no value. His strength comes only as he learns to work for and with others. The basketball superstar is extremely important to the team. But he cannot play a rival team all alone. We are at our best when we celebrate our individuality in the context of the group. And that is what economics is all about—people working together to meet needs that cannot be met alone.

But this book is not about economics as it is carried forward today. What we don't need is more of what we have. Your concern—like mine and that of millions of others in this country—is for an economy that works. All of us are appalled by what we've seen in recent years: spiraling inflation, high unemployment, the healthcare crisis, business and bank failures, recession, and the "D" word that professional economists run from—depression.

We are all painfully aware of the social fallout of a failing economy—crime, violence, divorce, drugs, illiteracy, poor health and poor healthcare. And what further unnerves us is that, with all their scientific equipment and know-how, all that professional economists can predict is a bleak and dismal picture of the future. It doesn't matter what political party the economists side with, they all predict the same—doom and gloom. We surely don't need any more depressing news. Is there any economic system with a brighter, more hopeful picture? I believe there is—and we will be considering it in the pages ahead.

Studying the works of leading economists has always left me depressed and hopeless. They paint a graphic picture of our economic dilemma backed by accurate statistics. But they have no real solutions.

In my search for something better, I've discovered a new economic system which I call Theo-Economics. This economic system foresees a far brighter and more hopeful picture. Unlike human economic systems, Theo-Economics focuses on possibilities—not on impossibilities. It sees the problems, but refuses to be stopped by them. This economy looks beyond the problems to the answers. It brings hope and security. Isn't this what millions like you and me have been looking for?

The term "Theo-Economics" is derived from three Greek words: *theo*, meaning God; *oikos*, meaning house or household; and *nomos*, meaning law or management. Joining the two words *oikos* and *nomos*, we come up with the word *oikonomia*, or the English word *economy*. Add *theo* to *oikonomia*, and we have the compound word *Theo-Economics*.

To some this might seem strange or even sacrilegious — placing God on the front of economy. But I can assure you that as you read on, you will discover, as I have, the reality and validity of Theo-Economics. This is not an ordinary economy. It is what I call a supra-economy. That is, it is an economy over, above, and beyond human economics. Theo-Economics conveys three powerful ideas:

1. God is in charge.
2. Management is mandatory.
3. Responsibility is required.

God Is in Charge

What a mental relief and assurance it is to know and believe that God is in charge. Not believing in a Supreme Being can bring on fear. And fear has caused many to fail and has kept millions from prospering. Many Americans are shaking in their boots. You can see the fear written on their faces. You can hear it in their voices. You can feel the tension when money issues are discussed.

This fear destroys the productive spirit. No one starts a business who is paralyzed by fear. How many will venture into unknown territory alone? Fear vanishes when the existence and presence of God are acknowledged.

Knowing that a Supreme Being is at the helm of the economy does indeed relieve stress.

> "So do not fear, for I am with you, do not be dismayed, for I am your God. I will strengthen you and help you; I will uphold you with my righteous right hand" (Isaiah 41:10).

King David came to believe in this supra-economy and wrote: "I was young and now I am old, yet I have never seen the righteous forsaken or their children begging bread" (Psalm 37:25). He understood fear. He experienced losses and financial reverses and settled the fear issues in these words:

> "I lift up my eyes to the hills — where does my help come from? My help comes from the Lord, the Maker of heaven and earth. He will not let your foot slip — he who watches over Israel will neither slumber nor sleep. The Lord watches over

you—the Lord is your shade at your right hand; the sun will not harm you by day nor the moon by night. The Lord will keep you from all harm—he will watch over your life; the Lord will watch over your coming and going both now and forevermore" (Psalm 121:1-8).

David was convinced that there was and is an economy beyond man. As the leader of a great nation, he saw the workings of human economy in the heathen nations around him. But experience made him a believer in Theo-Economics—an economy with God at its base. So convicted of God's sovereignty was David that he wrote, "The fool says in his heart 'There is no God'" (Psalm 14:1)

Denis Waitley, in his book, *Timing Is Everything*,[2] defines FEAR with this acronym:

F - **F**alse
E - **E**ducation
A - **A**ppearing
R - **R**eal

I truly believe we have been misinformed about God in today's society. Many have been educated to believe that God is behind church walls—that He is a part of some denomination. Or that if there is a God, He is not really concerned about our material welfare. This false education gives people the idea that they have to make it in life all alone. Added to this false information about God is the concept of rugged individualism—the idea that I must pick myself up by my own bootstraps.

No wonder so many are fearful. Who has the courage to walk through life alone? Rambo was just a movie character! Even John Wayne, in real life, didn't take everything on single-handedly.

The knowledge that God is in charge brings a sense of security. It gives us the courage to take risks, to face hard times, to confront disappointments, to venture into uncharted waters. Of course, there are those who pooh-pooh the idea of God. They do not believe in a real, supernatural power. With those, I feel no burden to argue the existence of God. In fact, God Himself doesn't try to prove His existence. You either believe it—or you don't. If we want to believe in God, there is enough evidence in nature and in the world to be convinced. Cliff Albritton, in his book, *Dare to Win! How To Live The American Dream!* writes:

> "The Person behind every life, the Sustainer of every soul and the true Source of every success is the unseen Spirit of the Universe. While there are those who doubt, those who are skeptical and others who oppose this reality, there is abundant evidence of the existence of God displayed in most if not all the natural sciences. Some of the greatest and most highly educated people in our sophisticated, scientific world personally believe in God and have had a personal relationship with Him."[3]

This idea of God being in charge makes Theo-Economics attractive. With God at the front of anything, it is bound to be successful.

Management Is Mandatory

To live in God's economy means to become a steward—a manager. This concept of stewardship, or management, is at the very root of economics. Again, the Greek word *oikonomia*, "economics," literally means "house-law." It means living in someone else's house and living by their rules. Theo-Economics is man living in God's house and abiding by His rules. This world is God's house—He privately owns it.

> "I am God, your God . . . for every animal of the forest is mine, and the cattle on a thousand hills. I know every bird in the mountains, and the creatures of the field are mine. If I were hungry I would not tell you, for the world is mine, and all that is in it" (Psalm 50:10-12).

God's ownership of the world places us in the position of being managers. Not owners—just plain managers! The secret of success in Theo-Economics, then, is not outdoing the next person but faithful stewardship—using our God-given abilities and talents as best we can.

Stewardship is a familiar term these days. Groups meet to discuss the stewardship or proper management of earth's natural resources. Even in the business world, the concept of stewardship has caught on. In the 1991 financial news, a reference was made to "the stewardship of the $16 billion Fidelity Magellan Fund" — the nation's largest stock fund, as it changed hands. In *The New York Times* during the period of 1986 and 1987, references were made to "concern about the stewardship of America's great corporate bureaucracies," to "Mrs. Thatcher's economic stewardship" in Great Britain, to Mayor Koch's "first steps toward redeeming his stewardship" in New York City after a scandal, to the head of the U.S. Internal Revenue Service ending "the longest stewardship of any commissioner since World War II," and even to "the stewardship of tradition" in baseball exercised by the clubhouse attendant of the New York Yankees.

No longer is the word *stewardship* confined to the weekly giving of church people. Many are becoming aware that maximizing human potential and natural resources is both profitable and wise.

Theo-Economics mandates management, because men are moral beings. A significant part of the "image of God" in man is the ability and freedom to makes choices. We can choose to live prosperous lives by faithful stewardship — or we can experience failure by poor management of our resources and abilities. The choice is ours.

The concept of stewardship is built on a higher view of man. We are more than merely higher life forms. We are created in the "image of God." Animals can be satisfied with food and maybe a place to live. But we human beings can never be satisfied with just having our material needs met. We are three dimensional. We have three different aspects to our lives: spiritual, mental, and physical (including the material). Proper stewardship demands the development of all three dimensions. Therefore, Theo-Economics, unlike human economics, is more concerned with people than with profits. It understands that filling man's belly is not good enough. "Man does not live by bread alone" (Deuteronomy 8:3; Matthew 4:4). Stewardship becomes a call to responsibility.

Responsibility Is Required

Responsibility is a natural outgrowth of stewardship. Responsibility is as natural to proper stewardship as oxygen is to air. No one can prosper in Theo-Economics without taking responsibility for his or her life. But it seems that few want to do this. The masses seem content to drift along, allowing others to decide their destiny. I am stunned by the many who spend their lives blaming others, circumstances, or their situations for their misfortunes. When the truth is told, they have failed to take charges of their lives.

And what is even more sad, human economic systems feed this irresponsibility. Modern economics, by the creation of welfare programs, prevents people from suffering the consequences of their bad decisions and out-of-control living. But Theo-Economics stops the drifting. It makes every steward responsible for his own ship. It requires each person to steer his own human vessel to the harbor of safety, happiness, and prosperity. It allows people to live with their personal choices. It brings what we have come to appreciate in this great country of ours — *freedom*. Freedom is the ability to make our own choices and live with the consequences. It is doing what we have decided is best. It is being accountable for our actions. Theo-Economics is a call to true freedom; thus it is a call to responsible living.

Human economics has as it purpose simply the production and distribution of goods to meet material needs. And in supplying those needs, "the greatest good for the greatest number" is considered the highest goal. But implied in this approach of supplying goods to meet needs is the idea that there are some who will fall between the cracks, that everybody can't win, that there are some losers. This philosophy bothers me. Who are the losers? Why can't everybody be a winner? Are there not enough resources to go around?

In Theo-Economics, there is a threefold purpose for economy.

1. Prosperity open to all.
2. Unity encouraged among all.
3. Eternity planned for all.

Prosperity Open to All

Theo-Economics views prosperity as available to all. No barriers exist to keep out those who honestly seek after prosperity. "The greatest good for everyone" is the idea of Theo-Economics. Jesus, the Son of God, holds out this promise for those who enter God's economy. "I have come that they might have life, and have it to the full," He says (John 10:10). Even though man has three dimensions, he is only one unit. Therefore, this promise covers every area of life.

The God of Theo-Economics is the God of plenty. There is no scarcity with God. Therefore, we need not fear that resources will run out. There may be shortages in man's economy, but never in the economy of God. God assures prosperity to all who enter His economy. "And God will supply all your needs according to His glorious riches in Christ Jesus" (Philippians 4:19). In Theo-Economics, prosperity is open to all.

Unity Encouraged Among All

In today's world, the individual is elevated above the group. In fact, the selfish pursuit of prosperity by individuals is seen as the motor that drives the economy. Success — not service — becomes the concern of contemporary economics. Staying at the front of the pack is the goal of those who live in this human economy. Competition — not cooperation — is rewarded. But Theo-Economics, unlike human economics, is grounded in unselfish service to man. It encourages cooperation among people. It acknowledges the brotherhood of all people and sees unity as one of its major goals. Human beings are part of one family; therefore, servicing needs should result in bringing people together instead of driving them apart.

The competitive spirit encouraged by modern economics does nothing more than further alienate people. This "me against the world" philosophy so prominent today drives huge wedges between people. It encourages separateness. On the other hand, Theo-Economics sees economics as a method of bringing people together. As people reach out to help others, mutual benefit is realized. Everybody wins. Stephen Covey, in his book, *Principle-Centered Leadership*, explains the 14 points of W. Edward Deming's Total Quality Principles:

> "He discusses in his 'Forces of Destruction' the past scripting of Win-Lose experiences received in school, sports, family,

politics, business, and education as competition rather than co-operation reigns throughout our society. In any interdependent relationship, thinking win-win is essential to long-term effectiveness. It requires an abundance mentality, an attitude that says, 'There is enough for all.' It cultivates the genuine desire to see the other party win as well, the orientation that any relationship should seek mutual benefit for all concerned. Deming believes that our society's competitive, win-lose paradigm is largely responsible for the problems in American management (economics)."[4]

Therefore, Theo-Economics encourages unity among people.

Eternity Planned for All

And finally, Theo-Economics focuses beyond this world. The goal of Theo-Economics is to prepare people to live eternally. It refuses to take the short view of life that contemporary economists take. It understands that this human economy is only temporary. The production and distribution of material supplies to meet needs on earth is just a break in the eternal economy of God. The plans and goals of Theo-Economics always anticipate a time beyond time as we know it now. Theo-Economics takes the word of the Jew of Nazareth seriously:

"Do not let your hearts be troubled. Trust in God, trust also in me. In my Father's house are many rooms; if it were not so, I would have told you. I am going there to prepare a place for you. And if I go and prepare a place for you, I will come back and take you to be with me that you also may be where I am" (John 14:1-3).

To the skeptics who may read these last few lines, I would say that this should be the great hope of all of us. It was indeed the hope of many of our founding fathers. Benjamin Franklin, realizing that God is above all human economy, wrote that "God will certainly reward virtue and punish vice, either here or hereafter."

Franklin, along with many of the founding fathers, anticipated a time when human economy would be completely overtaken by God's economy. Therefore, Theo-Economics makes provision for everyone who enters this God-based economy to enjoy eternity.

I believe that no scheme of business or plan of life can be sound or complete that embraces only the brief years of this present life and makes no provision for the unending future. That is the purpose of Theo-Economics.

2

The Language of Economy

Not long ago, I asked a recent college graduate this question: "What comes to your mind when you hear the word *economics*?"

After a thoughtful pause, she replied, "Well, I think of balance sheets, budgets, debits, and those money terms that I don't understand."

"When you think of economics, what type of people come to your mind?" I quizzed her further.

"Of course, professional economists—experts. Aren't they the only ones involved in economics?"

This young graduate's response echoes the impressions of the vast majority of people. Many feel that economics should be left to the experts. And the experts seem to like it that way. Their technical language acts as a barrier to keep all but the experts out.

It is not uncommon to create a language to communicate new concepts. We see this done every day and in all walks of life. Plumbers, electricians, contractors, and even religious groups have their language and vocabulary that only people who are a part of the discipline can understand.

A couple of years ago when I entered the academic arena, I had the privilege of attending my first theological society meeting. What an experience! As I entered the dining area where the theologues had gathered, I was ambushed by the intelligentsia. I first had to give my pedigree (what degree I hold), and of course, my area of expertise and the school where I received my graduate training. I survived this assault, but as I listened to the first paper being presented, I knew then that I was on another planet. I felt like asking my friend who was with me what language the speaker was speaking, because I only understood a word here and there—mostly there!

After nearly two decades as a pastor, the language of the theologian was almost foreign to me. Of course, I had done my share of theological reading, but I found no practical use for the language in my work among the lay people in churches under my charge. Can you image how well a sermon on "Forensic Justification" or on the "Teleological Argument for God" would have gone over in a little church of working people in small-town America? I can assure you, not very well.

Now, to be sure, I did preach on profound theological issues, but I always couched the messages in the language of the people. If I hadn't, I would not have had a job!

The purpose of language is to communicate thoughts and feelings to others through the human voice. And communication only takes place when understanding of meanings occurs between people. What seems to have taken place on the economic front of this nation is the exclusion of American citizens from economic discussions by the creation of a new technical language. Economics is now discussed solely among the experts. And when the regular taxpayer seeks to enter into the dialogue, he is told he doesn't understand or is made to feel ignorant by the onslaught of high-browed terminology familiar only to the "experts."

I really understand how the regular taxpayer must feel, for as I sat there among the theologians in that most memorable meeting, I felt out of place, stupid, ignorant, and dared not say a word. I felt as if I had nothing to contribute. They were the "experts." But what we must come to understand is that the work of economics is the work of every citizen of this nation. Everyone can make a contribution.

Theo-Economics, on the other hand, values the insights of all people. The Bible declares the worth of all men. It proclaims the God of the Bible as unbiased and willing to communicate through any and all who will allow Him to. Economic answers ultimately come from God. Therefore, God chooses whom He will to provide answers to our economics woes. Sometimes He gives answers through the experts. But sometimes He passes by the economists and communicates to the common man.

> "But God chose the foolish things of the world to shame the wise; God chose the weak things of the world to shame the strong. He chose the lowly things of this world and the despised things — and the things that are not — to nullify the things that are, so that no one may boast before him" (1 Corinthians 1:27-29).

It appears that human economics isn't interested in what the little man has to say. But in God's economy, every person is of value. Everyone can make a contribution to the production, distribution, and maintenance of the economic system.

In my years as a leader, I have seen people with little formal education come up with the most profound and effective solutions to financial dilemmas. I have also had the sad experience of hearing businessmen and economists talking the highbrow language of economics while leading organizations down the tube. All across this country, we are witnessing the failure of businesses and organizations led by the "experts."

It has become increasingly clear to me that economics is not about words — but about action. Not about espousing high-sounding theories — but about seeing root causes and clear solutions and having the courage to act. It's about hunches and feelings and impressions. It's about understanding human nature. It's about finding simple solutions to very difficult issues. In this new economy, we say it's about hearing the voice of God and being willing to hear God speak through whomever He chooses.

Henry Ford knew nothing about economics. In fact, he had very little formal education. Yet he became the richest man in America. Henry Ford operated from what he called hunches. His hunches were based on his sensitivity to the needs of working people. As he sought to meet the needs of the common man, his economic theories evolved. He worked from the principle that laborers were customers too, and he defied the economists of his day by paying his workers $5.00 minimum per day in wages. His idea for the mass production of economical cars and his fair treatment of workers through payment of high wages and good benefits changed the face, not only of the American economy, but of the world economy as well.

Mr. Ford was never able to express in economic language the theories that made his company such a huge success. But in 1926, collaborating with Samuel Crowther in the book *Today and Tomorrow,* he did write out his economic philosophy. Perhaps Mr. Ford's idea was, "Let me work out my hunch. If it works, then let's try to put it into words."

Henry Ford was not an economist and never became an economist. And even though he had around him economists and other learned men, he knew that ideas don't just come from the "experts." He understood that it is good, most of the time, to follow your heart. In reading the recent literature of business today, it is clear that a move is on to include more working people in the discussion of production, distribution, and problem solving. Industry has been forced to face the fact that often the man on the line knows better how to solve mechanical and production problems than the "expert." He may not know how to express it in words, but he knows what needs to be done.

But as industry moves in the direction of including more people in the discussion of the production process, we haven't seen that in the broader field of economics. There, the idea still seems to prevail that the little people don't know much. That idea is communicated clearly: "You people be good citizens and pay your taxes, but we don't need your input." And wasn't it just that kind of philosophy that brought on the American revolution? People expressing their need to be heard about how the economy should be run—about taxation without representation. People are smart enough to know that they don't have all the answers to a complex economy such as the one we live in. But they do want to feel that in some way, even if in just a small way, they can help with the economic problems of this country. I believe that the exclusion of the regular citizen by the use of this new technical economic language has closed the door of participation to the very ones who could just possibly have the answers to our economic woes.

An old, wise man once said:

> "Now there lived in that city a man poor but wise, and saved the city by his wisdom. But nobody remembered that poor man. So I said, Wisdom is better than strength [degrees]. But the poor man's wisdom is despised, and his words are no longer heeded" (Ecclesiastes 9:6).

Including people in the economic discussion begins by teaching the general public the language of economics, not necessarily by changing the language—even though that might not be a bad idea. Just as we expect all Americans to learn English, we should expect all to learn the language of economy.

Theo-Economics intentionally keeps its language plain, simple, and straight-forward. The simplicity of the language makes it available to everyone, thus encouraging all to participate in the economic system. In the language of Theo-Economics, there are only thirteen essential terms or words:

1. **God**—the Supreme Being in charge of the economy.
2. **Faith**—belief and confidence in both God and man.
3. **Responsibility**—taking charge of one's life. Being accountable for one's actions.
4. **Diligence**—careful, constant, and persistent effort in doing a job.
5. **Honesty**—the characteristic of sincerity and fairness. Not lying, cheating, or over-reaching in business.

6. **Self-denial** — the willingness to put self and self-interest aside for the good of others. Putting off immediate gratification for future goals and benefits.

7. **Thrift** — consciousness about waste, with an eye toward prosperity.

8. **Temperance** — self-restraint and control in every area of life. The complete abandonment of all indulgent practices.

9. **Tithe** — 10 percent of one's increase, placed back in organizations that teach and live the message of the Bible.

10. **Alms** — freewill offerings given to humanitarian projects that meet the needs of suffering people or that are invested for the uplifting of humanity.

11. **Saving** — putting money aside for future goals and emergencies.

12. **Investment** — putting money and energy into one's personal gifts, talents, and abilities.

13. **Purity** — freedom from evil surmising and scheming — and living within God's laws.

In Theo-Economics, these thirteen words are really thirteen principles. Once the words are learned and lived by, success is guaranteed. God Himself becomes responsible for the results. There is no anxiety in God's economy. The practice of diligence, fidelity, care-taking, thrift, and discretion will always be rewarded by God.

"And without faith it is impossible to please God, because anyone who comes to him must believe that he exists and that he rewards those who earnestly seek him" (Hebrews 11:6).

In Theo-Economics, as mentioned earlier, we are not called to be successful but to be faithful. Therefore, our dependence will be, not on the success of our efforts, but on the promises of God.

"So do not worry, saying 'what shall we eat?' or 'What shall we drink?' or 'What shall we wear?' . . . But seek first his kingdom and his righteousness, and all these things will be given to you as well" (Matthew 6:31-33).

Notice that the language (or principles) of Theo-Economics

begins with God. Recognition of God and His ownership of the world lies at the foundation of business integrity and of true success. Bound up with these thirteen principles is the well-being of society—both secular and religious. These principles give security to property and life. For all that makes confidence and cooperation possible, the world is indebted to these principles that come out of the economy of God and are used by men in other human economies, whether consciously or unconsciously.

I believe that every citizen should have the chance to know the language of human economic systems. Economic illiteracy and ignorance is not bliss—but bust. My concern is not so much learning the language in order to succeed, but knowing human systems well enough to determine how they affect us.

I've taken New Testament Greek. My purpose in learning it was not to prepare myself to speak the language, but to know it well enough to interpret the New Testament for myself. Learning the language of human economy makes us better able to interpret what goes on around us. Therefore, I have included thirty economic terms, that if learned, will help in discussing the human economics that affects everyone's life.

Economics Terms

1. **Economics**—the study of how people work together to supply their material needs.
2. **Resources**—the things that go into the making of goods and services. There are three types of resources:
   A. **Natural resources**—those things provided by nature.
   B. **Human resources**—people who, with their brain power and muscle, put everything together.
   C. **Capital resources**—the machines, tools, money, and buildings used in the production of goods and services.
3. **Supply**—the amount of goods or services available for sale at a particular price.
4. **Demand**—how much of goods or services people will buy at a particular price.
5. **Consumer**—anyone who buys goods or services for his or her own use.

6. **Producer** — a person who makes and sell the things people buy.

7. **Ecological concern** — concern for saving the environment, preserving unspoiled areas, and rescuing polluted areas.

8. **Direct sales** — selling supplies directly to consumers.

9. **Advertising** — reaching the consumer through the mass media (radio, television, newspapers, magazines).

10. **Packaging** — wrapping and boxing supplies in an attractive manner, to entice consumers to buy.

11. **Credit** — a form of borrowing. An IOU.

12. **Installment buying** — buying an item and paying for it over a specified period of time by making monthly or weekly payments.

13. **Garnisheeing** — attachment of one's wages or salary by court order in payment of a debt.

14. **Finance charge** — the total of all charges you must pay on an installment or regular loan.

15. **Annual percentage rate (APR)** — the interest paid on a loan over a year's time. A 12 percent APR equals 1 percent monthly on the unpaid balance of a loan.

16. **Unpaid balance** — the amount owed after a payment is made on a charge account. This amount declines with each payment.

17. **Gross national product (GNP)** — the total value of all the goods and services produced in a country in a single year.

18. **Deficit spending** — borrowing money to meet expenses.

19. **Inflation** — an increase in the money supply, which elevates costs and devalues money in circulation.

20. **Consumer price index** — a method of measuring the prices consumers pay for the the things they buy.

21. **Recession** — a short decline in the level of business activity.

22. **Depression** — a long period of decline in the level of business.

23. **Full employment** — the situation that prevails when everyone who would like to have a job is able to find one.

24. **Business cycle** — the movement of business from good times to bad and back again.

24. **Monetary policy**—the government's use of its power to tax and spend in order to influence the business cycle.

25. **Fiscal policy**—the government's use of its power to increase or decrease the supply of money in order to influence the business cycle.

26. **Imports**—goods and services purchased from foreign countries.

27. **Exports**—goods and services sold to countries abroad.

28. **Tariff**—a tax on imports.

29. **Stocks**—certificates issued to people who share in the ownership of a corporation.

30. **Bonds**—certificates issued by the government and by private corporations to those who lend them money.

This is not, of course, an exhaustive list. I recommend you get a high school economics textbook and study it for further information. ⇨ ⇨ ⇨ ⇨ ⇨ ⇨ ⇨ ⇨

A Message to Wall Street, Politicians, and Economists

We value your training, experience, and leadership, but please tear down the barriers to communication that have been erected by your economic terminology. Speak in words we can understand, and teach us your language as you go along. We don't mind you talking among yourselves — just don't forever leave us out. We don't know everything, but we do know something. We do have brains, and we use them to think about our economic problems. Stop by the barber shop, beauty shop, or just walk through the grocery store, and listen to us; you may find we have something to offer. We love our country, too, and want the best for it.

A Message to the Grass Roots

You are valuable to this country. Every vote, every opinion, every dollar is needed to keep our nation moving in the right direction. Do not allow experts to intimidate you. Use your brain. We need you to help solve our national economic crisis. "For lack of guidance a nation fails, but many advisers make victory sure" (Proverbs 11:14). But don't be satisfied with your own limited knowledge of economics. Read! Read! Read! Take time to learn the language of the economist. You may never be able to have a running conversation with the experts, but at least you will be able to follow them.

Early in my ministry, I was involved in my first building project. It was a small church in a small town. I had never built anything in my life. This was an all-new experience. Completely ignorant of building, I went to the library, checked out a half dozen books on the building trade, and locked myself in my office at home to learn the language of building. I then visited many different kinds of church facilities, getting ideas. Armed with ideas from many different church plants, I then sat down to sketch out what kind of facility I thought my congregation needed.

Amazingly, with no drafting experience and no artistic ability, I was able to sketch out a plan on paper. My sketch wouldn't have won a contest, but it was clear and detailed enough to give to a contractor. My sketch was good enough that the contractor was able to build from it. Now, I don't recommend you try what I did. I do believe a good architect is worth his weight in gold. But what I am saying is, take the time to increase your knowledge about economics. It will pay big dividends down the road. With solid information, you can follow your hunches without fear.

3

The Invisible Hand

I made a decision several years ago, based on my understanding of the Bible, to live a debt-free life. This placed me in the position of using credit as a last option in handling financial matters. At that point, my old Lincoln Town Car decided to fall apart. In fact, on what became its final out-of-town trip (we kept the car for another three years while we got out of debt), the car broke down two hundred miles away from home. The repair estimate was $1,000.00.

We had $600.00 in our checking accounts, and we had not finished paying all our bills. We knew that once the bills were paid, even that money would be gone. Adding to this dilemma, we had only a small reserve in the bank. And when I say a small reserve, that is what I mean.

Since my wife and I had made the commitment not to borrow, we decided to work this one out with the help of the "Invisible Hand." Experiences in our earlier years of marriage had taught us that God could be trusted. As we balanced our checkbook, we knew, humanly speaking, that our checking account could not absorb a $1,000.00 auto repair bill.

But to our delight, as we entered the last of the checks, which included the check for $1,000.00, our account still showed a balance of $175.00. There was no prior miscalculation in our checking account. We had no room in our budget for mistakes, so we made sure the checkbook stayed balanced to the penny. Neither was there a banking error. There were no generous benefactors or accidental deposits. All we know is that the Unseen Watcher, knowing our desire to leave a debt-free life, decided to become involved in our financial affairs and added $400.00 to our checking account.

This chapter is not about religious beliefs or mysticism. It is about a reality—the reality of an "Invisible Hand" that is involved in the personal and corporate economics of this nation. As you study the history of this country, you will discover, as I have, that there are many inexplicable occurrences that have brought this nation to where it is today.

How do we explain the emergence of thirteen financially, militarily, and numerically weak states into the wealthiest and most powerful nation in the world? Do we honestly believe it was done solely through our founding fathers' ingenuity, determination, and strength? Our founding fathers didn't think so. That is why, on October 14, 1795, Samuel Adams, then the governor of Massachusetts, proclaimed Thursday, the nineteenth day of November, as a day of public thanksgiving and praise.

Adams acknowledged in this declaration that it was God who united the states; who kept internal peace among the thirteen colonies; who caused the earth to yield abundantly, the fishing industry to prosper, and trading to flourish despite tremendous opposition; who kept wars from the land and gave wisdom to the leaders to provide a constitution that protects each citizen's rights, liberty, and privileges.[1] It was clear to these early pioneers that a divine force was at work to bring prosperity to this nation.

Modern economists are aware that there is an inexplicable, uncontrollable force at work in the economy. But their identification of this force is inconsistent with Theo-Economics. Adam Smith, considered to be the father of our nation's modern economic theory, used the term "The Invisible Hand" to describe this force. He viewed "The Invisible Hand" as competition in a free market system. He believed that the unencumbered trade of a free market system would regulate the flow of wealth.

Smith was well aware of the selfish nature of man. But he believed that if people were allowed to pursue their selfish goals and accumulate wealth, competition among suppliers would keep selfishness in check.

Smith was wrong in his conclusions about competition. Competition doesn't help — it hurts. When does selfishness lead to supporting? When does competition view competitors as compatriots? Yet our country bought into Smith's philosophy, and now we are feeling the bitter stings of a selfish society. The conspicuous consumption of the rich and the want-to-be-rich in this country tells the story of an economic system gone wrong. Competition appears at first to serve the best interests of American citizens. But in the end, it kills off the weak and the struggling, leaving only the strong to survive.

We protest the murder of millions of unborn babies through abortion, while praising a system that slaughters millions of unborn or weak potential producers through competition. A group of modern economists, however, having seen the failure of Smith's "Invisible Hand" idea, deny the existence of any Unseen Force. They believe in the quite visible and aggressive hand of management and entrepreneurship to keep the economy moving and balanced. With high-tech advertisement, sophisticated theories, and high-powered computers, they seek to control the economy — but to no avail. We still have recession and rising unemployment.

What few — including modern economists — fail to understand is that economics is not a science but a philosophy. And a philosophy is controlled by what one believes, or better still, in whom one believes. Because modern economists have failed to identify God as this "Invisible Hand," they cannot foresee an end in the downward plunge of our economy.

Theo-Economics, on the other hand, can pierce through the dark clouds of economic depression and see a silver lining. It can do this because of its philosophical underpinnings. In looking at man's economic condition, Theo-Economics begins with man's spiritual condition. The selfish nature of man that Adam Smith speaks about in his economic theories is nothing more than man's sinful nature, developed as a result of his violation of God's laws. So now man, by nature, is lawless. He is out of control.

Theo-Economics believes that bad economics is perpetuated by the sinful nature of man. In fact, a quick examination of our bad economic picture reveals the destructive forces of greed, selfishness, lying, cheating, stealing, and the lust after power and money—all of which are the outworkings of man's corrupt nature. To stop these destructive forces will take more than human theories, calculation, and power—it will take God. That is why Theo-Economics places its trust in the "Invisible Hand" of God, intervening in human economy.

Theo-Economics believes that any other solution to man's economic problems, apart from God, is like putting a bandage on a gaping sore. "Can the Ethiopian change his skin, or the leopard its spots? Neither can you do good who are accustomed to doing evil" (Jeremiah 13:23). Man, left to himself, will not only continue to bring ruin to the economy but will soon self-destruct. Yet divine intervention into human affairs can remedy even the worst of economic conditions. "With God all things are possible" (Matthew 19:26).

No wonder the Theo-Economist can have such an optimistic outlook on economic conditions! No wonder he can see a silver lining through the thick black clouds of economic despair. He does not deny the bleak economic picture. But he refuses to see the case as hopeless. God is that "Invisible Hand" that controls the world. And again, this world belongs to God.

"The Mighty One, God, the Lord, speaks and summons the earth from the rising of the sun to the place where it sets. For every animal of the forest is mine and the cattle on a thousand hills, and the creatures of the field are mine. If I were hungry I would not tell you, for the world is mine, and all that is in it. The silver and gold is mine, saith the Lord" (Psalm 50:1, 10-12; Haggai 2:8).

God makes Himself directly responsible for what happens in this world.

I would hope that many of today's economists do believe in God, but perhaps they feel like a man who asked me, "Do you really think God makes people wealthy?" In other words, Do you really think God gets His hands dirty in the affairs of man? This view of God is what we call, in theological circles, deistic. This deistic view of God acknowledges His existence, but views Him as an absentee landlord. God did create the world, deists believe. They maintain He wound it up like a precision-made clock. Then He went off on some eternal picnic, leaving the world to run on its own. This view essentially says that God doesn't care what happens to the world. What a grim picture of God! No wonder human economics is falling apart. Man really believes he must and can run the economy without God.

Moses, the leader of one of the greatest nations in earth's history, wrote, as he thought about his own nation's prosperity, "But remember the Lord your God, for it is he who gives you the ability to produce wealth, and so confirms his covenant, which he sware to your forefathers, as it is today" (Deuteronomy 8:18). Moses clearly recognized God's hand in the prosperity of the nation. He discovered a personal God who holds Himself ultimately responsible for the world.

God's ultimate ownership of the earth places Him at the heart of Theo-Economics. He becomes a personal power player in economic affairs, particularly of those who enter this new economy as well as that of the nation. He is called the "Invisible Hand" by Theo-Economists, because He is unseen, yet His hand is felt and experienced in the economy. The Theo-Economist sees God as both "Immanent" and "Transcendant." (Of course, I could not write this book without using *some* of those high-brow terms theologians use!)

Transcendant means that God is supreme, sovereign, preeminent, and stands out and above man. *Immanent* conveys the meaning of closeness, of intimacy, of God's presence in the world. God is right here with us. He is involved in our lives. Those who accept Theo-Economics find the involvement of God in the economy assuring and consoling.

To know that an omnipotent (all-powerful), omniscient (all-knowing), and omnipresent (everywhere at all times) God is active in the affairs of the nation is reassuring. To believe that we are not left to the fickle finger of competition or the capricious hand of entrepreneurs and management is comforting. For those of us who buy into Theo-Economics, spiraling inflation, out-of-control budgets, and high unemployment do not frighten us. We know that the "Invisible Hand" is in control.

This was not a foreign idea to the founding fathers of this nation. Benjamin Franklin wrote, as his life's creed, "I believe in God, Creator of the universe. That He governs it by His providence." When the leaders of the United States assembled to write the constitution, Benjamin Franklin proposed that each session be opened with prayer. He said, "I have lived a long time, and the longer I live, the more convincing proof I see of this truth—that God governs the affairs of men. And if a sparrow cannot fall to the ground without His notice, is it possible that an empire can rise without His aid?"

These national patriarchs were convinced that an Unseen Being was active in the affairs of the nation. George Washington, first president of the United States, cried out as he stood in the snow at the battle of Valley Forge, "The event is in the hands of God." As the battle grew worse and the tide of the battle turned against his men, he said, "How will it end? God will direct."

A personal friend of Abraham Lincoln wrote about his stay with the president at the White House during the Civil War:

> "I had been spending three weeks with Mr. Lincoln as his guest. One night—it was just after the battle of Bull Run—I was restless and could not sleep. . . . from the private room where the president slept, I heard low tones, for the door was partly open. Instinctively, I wandered in, and there I saw a sight which I have never forgotten. It was the president, kneeling before an open Bible . . . his back toward me. I shall never forget his prayer: 'Oh, Thou God, that heard Solomon in the night when he prayed and cried for wisdom, hear me. I cannot lead these people, I cannot guide the affairs of this nation without Thy help . . . O God, hear me and save this nation.'"[2]

A prophetic historian, reflecting on the Civil War, wrote these words:

"I had a view of the disastrous battle at Manassas, Virginia. It was a most exciting, distressing scene. The Southern army had everything in their favor and were prepared for a dreadful contest. The Northern army was moving on with triumph, not doubting but that they would be victorious. Many were reckless and marched forward boastingly, as though victory were already theirs. As they neared the battlefield, many were almost fainting through weariness and want of refreshment. They did not expect so fierce an encounter. They rushed into battle and fought bravely, desperately. The dead and dying were on every side. Both the North and the South suffered severely. The Southern men felt the battle, and in a little while would have been driven back still further. The Northern men were rushing on, although their destruction was very great. Just then an angel descended and waved his hand backward. Instantly there was confusion in the ranks. It appeared to the Northern men that their troops were retreating, when it was not so in reality, and a precipitate retreat commenced. This seemed wonderful to me.

"Then it was explained that God had this nation in His own hand, and would not suffer victories to be gained faster than He ordained, and would permit no more losses to the Northern men than in His wisdom He saw fit, to punish them for their sins. And had the Northern army at this time pushed the battle still further in their fainting, exhausted condition, the far greater struggle and destruction which awaited them would have caused great triumph in the South. God would not permit this, and sent an angel to interfere. The sudden falling back of the Northern troops is a mystery to all. They know not that God's hand was in the matter."[3]

Throughout the Bible, we see God's involvement in the affairs of man. In the Old Testament book of Daniel is the account of Nebuchadnezzar and his mysterious dream. Nebuchadnezzar is disturbed by a dream he can't remember, but he is sure it has some special meaning. The prophet Daniel is summoned after the king has failed to find answers from his own wise men (economists). After consulting with God, Daniel comes back with the dream and its interpretation. The dream chronicles the rise and fall of Babylon and other nations, underscoring the "Invisible Hand" of God as He leads the nation to its final destiny.

Nebuchadnezzar believed for a while in God's mighty hand in the affairs of the nation. But like many today, Nebuchadnezzar lost sight of the "Invisible Hand." He thought it was his intelligence, cleverness, and courage that prospered the kingdom. So God took his mind and left him in a demented state for seven years to show him who was in charge. Years later, Nebuchadnezzar's grandson Belshazzar, like many modern economists, also denied God's involvement in the affairs of the nation. So God chose to show His hand at a palace bash. As Belshazzar sat in a drunken stupor, God wrote on the ballroom wall words that unequivocally identified Him as the "Invisible Hand" who holds the destiny of all economies in His hand. Take time to read these stories in Daniel, chapters 2 through 5.

Another dramatic demonstration of God's active intervention in the economy of a nation is found in the story of Joseph. The Old Testament book of Genesis records the account of a great famine that struck Egypt and all the countries around. Joseph was called on, like Daniel, to interpret a dream that troubled the king. Again, the Unseen Watcher, God, revealed the future of the kingdom through a symbolic dream. The dream detailed seven years of prosperity followed by seven years of famine (depression).

Joseph, a prisoner, a shepherd, and not one of Pharaoh's wise men (economists), was pressed into service to prepare for the famine and later to manage the kingdom during this great depression. Through wisdom given him by God, millions were spared starvation, drought, and death. Read about this story in Genesis 39 through 41.

These biblical illustrations of God's intervention into the affairs of nations ratify — to the Theo-Economist and those who accept this view of God — the reality that God is involved in the affairs of men. These Bible incidents show that even though God has His own economy, human economy is affected by His economy. To deny the intrusion of the "Invisible Hand" of God into human economics is like refusing to believe in electricity and therefore never turning on the switch to obtain light. To relegate the inexplicable to capricious competition or mercurial management is to deny the power of God available to this country and its citizens.

Check Point

■ There is an "Invisible Hand" in the world.

■ The "Invisible Hand" is not competition.

■ Competition is not compassionate but destructive.

■ The "Invisible Hand" is God.

■ Thanksgiving holiday is proof that our founding fathers believed in God's involvement in this nation's affairs.

■ We deny ourselves unlimited resources and power when we deny God's involvement in the world.

4

"I'm Tired of Being Poor"

Apart of my childhood was spent in the antebellum city of Savannah, Georgia. I recall sitting on the stoop of a friend's house that faced an unpaved street, arguing over who was the poorest. I would say, "I'm the poorest, and I spell *poor* with six o's!" He would fire back, "I'm the poorest, and I spell *poor* with ten o's!" This would sometimes go on for hours, with no agreement reached on who was indeed the poorest.

What a child's game! And for both of us, it was just that—a child's game. We were a long way from being rich, but we certainly were not poor. Both of us lived in decent houses. We had plenty to eat. I attended a private Christian school and never had to worry about my physical needs being met.

But real poverty is not a game. It is a horrifying reality in our country. Even though the poor in America are rich by comparison with the rest of the world's poor, it should not in any way minimize the plight of our nation's underprivileged.

Homelessness is terrible in any country. Being hungry in Chicago is just as bad as being hungry in Calcutta. The sinkhole of poverty is an atrocity in any land, language, or lineage.

Few scenes capture the heart as does the plight of the poor. I have seen the stress-filled faces of parents who worry about the next meal for their children. I have watched the depressed gait of the long-term unemployed. My heart has ached witnessing the ignorance, illiteracy, and hopelessness—the waste of human potential—in the neighborhoods of this land. The stark reality is that poverty is not prejudice. The deprived faces of the poor come in all shapes, sizes, and colors. Neither is poverty relegated to certain areas of our nation. From the sprawling cities to the backwoods of rural America comes the cry, "I am tired of being poor!"

What is poverty? Poverty is the condition of being without the necessities of life. It is being deprived of decent housing, adequate and nutritional food, proper medical care. It is living in ignorance. It is being deprived of human dignity. It is a condition that over thirty million people in this country are forced to live in every day. It a condition that cannot be escaped by any economic system. Poverty is a serious problem. For it not only drains the economy, it destroys the people in it.

Modern economists have been at a loss as to how to deal with this cancerous sore called poverty. Perhaps that is because they have often been more concerned with programs than with people. It seems as if concern too often begins with attempting to remedy the problem and then later worrying about the people.

Public housing in this country is illustrative of this "problem versus people" approach to dealing with poverty. Who asked the poor what kind of housing they wanted and needed? No one! Someone saw the problem. They designed a solution—thousands of high-rise apartments. Then they stuck the powerless poor in them. What a disaster! That solution only compounds the problems of the poor.

A good starting point for solving the problem of poverty in this country is to investigate its original cause. Contemporary economics has failed miserably here. It has no real reference point to begin an investigation of root causes. Theo-Economics, on the other hand, has the Bible, which clearly sets forth not only the original cause but shows when and where poverty began.

Poverty actually began, according to the Bible, over six thousand years ago, not long after man was created. But poverty was not man's original state. His original condition was one of prosperity. God placed him in the midst of a beautiful garden and put at his disposal everything his heart could ever desire. Yet the prosperity of man was conditional. So long as he obeyed the direct mandate of God not to eat of the tree of the knowledge of good and evil in the midst of the garden (see Genesis 2:9), he could retain his prosperous Edenic home.

But the perfect pair violated the command of God. Consequently, they forfeited not only their garden home but also their holy covering. They experienced the first eviction and the first loss of a shirt! Here is where poverty began. Even the earth was affected by the sin of Adam and Eve. A curse was placed on the earth, causing difficulty in tilling the soil. Thorns and thistles sprouted on flowers as a symbol of hard times—of poverty. Since the fall of our original parents, the world has become a lazar house of sin and poverty (see Genesis, chapters 2 and 3).

Theo-Economics sees poverty as a condition of man brought on by sin. Poverty is not sin, but a result of sin. Therefore, to rid the earth of poverty would be like saying, "Let's get together and rid the earth of sin." Jesus, speaking of the poor, said, "You will always have the poor among you" (John 12:8). He did not mean by His statement that we need do nothing to help the poor, but that curing poverty is beyond all human ability. Yet Jesus still taught by precept and example that we are under obligation to do whatever we can to eliminate poverty.

Sin is the general cause of poverty. But it is important that we examine poverty from three perspectives—the causes of poverty, the remedy for poverty, and the proper treatment of the poor.

The Causes of Poverty

1. External causes over which the poor have no control.

Leading the list of the causes of poverty is injustice and oppression. Oppressive government and grasping people strip whatever they can from the powerless — land, resources, and human dignity. The God of Theo-Economics speaks out against this evil. "What do you mean by crushing my people and grinding the faces of the poor? declares the Lord, the Lord Almighty" (Isaiah 3:15).

The Theo-Economist sees the plight of the poor as a call to action. Theo-Economics sees its job as speaking against greed, injustice, and oppression. Unlike modern economists, who dare not talk of ethical issues, Theo-Economists know that economics must always be ethical if it is to be just. They know that there can be no solution to poverty unless oppressive and unjust systems are dealt with.

Theo-Economics mandates responsibility — governmental and corporate responsibility. Racism, sexism, class-ism, unfair hiring practices, unjust laws, non-enforcement of just laws, all help to keep people in poverty.

Famine, accident, sickness, and death are also all causes of poverty that people have no control over. Many families have lost everything because of one or a number of these things. The Bible clearly states that this class of poor — those who suffer poverty through no cause of their own — deserve and need the help of outside sources.

2. Debt.

I will talk extensively about debt in a later chapter. But for now, we must see that debt plays a large part in keeping people in poverty in this country. All through history, people have been getting into trouble over indebtedness. And today's poor are no different. Carelessness, extravagance, and cavalier living lead many to borrow.

Studies show that poor people watch more television than any other socio-economic group. This is because many are unemployed, which allows them more free time to watch television. With limited money, television for the poor becomes a cheap form of entertainment.

But is television really a cheap form of entertainment? The average American family watches from five to six hours of television per day. They are confronted with about thirteen commercials during each half hour of programming. In one year, the average family has seen over forty thousand commercials. It must work. Corporate America is still investing billions in television commercials. And poor people are among the millions manipulated into buying on credit that which they can't afford—or spending money they do not have on non-essentials.

3. Ill-considered benevolence.

In the last two to three decades, many poor have been crippled by indiscriminate giving. Many programs designed to help the poor have done more harm than good. Many government, church, and charitable aid programs teach the poor to be dependent. These programs have good intentions but usually end up encouraging selfishness and helplessness. This often leads to idleness, extravagance, and intemperance. And these are the traits that shackle the poor to poverty.

4. Laziness.

I am very careful but specific here in calling some poor people lazy. There is an attitude about the poor that I believe is unwarranted and unfair. I will deal with this a little later. But I am well aware that there are those in poverty because they refuse to work. Many have been trained that way through social programs that require nothing more than that people come in and collect their benefits.

Others have never learned how to be industrious. Still others grow up believing that the world owes them a living, so they go around with their hands out and a chip on their shoulders. The Bible paints a graphic picture of the lazy man, along with the subsequent results: "A little sleep, a little slumber, a little folding of the hands to rest, and poverty will come on you like a bandit and scarcity like an armed man" (Proverbs 24: 33, 34).

Of all the causes of poverty, Solomon labels laziness as number one. Laziness is a sign that a person doesn't want to take responsibility for his life. He wants others to take care of him.

No one who can earn his own livelihood has a right to depend on others. The world owes no one a living who is able to work and gain a living for himself. The Bible clearly states, "If a man will not work, he shall not eat" (2 Thessalonians 3:10).

4. Alcohol, drugs, and cigarettes.

These vices have stolen billions of dollars out of the pockets of the poor. Money that should have been used to lift people out of the pits of degradation is blown on alcohol, drugs, and cigarettes. But not only have these vices stolen money, they have destroyed health, broken up homes, and taken the lives of innocent people. One writer puts it in these words:

> "Every year millions upon millions of intoxicating liquors are consumed. Millions upon millions of dollars are spent in buying wrenching poverty, disease, degradation, lust, crime, and death. For the sake of gain, the liquor seller deals out to his victims that which corrupts and destroys mind and body. He entails on the drunkard's family poverty and wretchedness.
>
> "When his victim is dead, the rum seller's exactions do not cease. He robs the widow and brings children to beggary. He does not hesitate to take the very necessaries of life from the destitute family, to pay the drink bill of the husband, and father. The cries of the suffering children, the tears of the agonized mother, serve only to exasperate him. What is it to him if these suffering ones starve? What is it to him if they, too, are driven to degradation and ruin? He grows rich on the pittances of those whom he is leading to perdition."[1]

What is said here about alcohol holds true for both drugs and cigarettes.

The Bible gives strong warning about liquor. "He who loves pleasure will become poor; whoever loves wine and oil will never be rich. . . . Wine is a mocker and beer a brawler; whoever is led astray by them is not wise" (Proverbs 21:17; 20: 1). But not only does the Bible give warnings, it even describes the plight of the drunkard.

> "Who has woe? Who has sorrow? Who has strife? Who has complaints? Who has needless bruises? Who has bloodshot

eyes? Those who linger over wine, who go to sample bowls of mixed wine. Do not gaze at wine when it is red, when it sparkles in the cup, when it goes down smoothly! In the end it bites like a snake and poisons like a viper. Your eyes will see strange sights and your mind imagine confusing things. You will be like one sleeping on the high seas, lying on top of the rigging. 'They hit me,' you will say, 'but I'm not hurt! They beat me, but I don't feel it! When will I wake up so I can find another drink?'" (Proverbs 23:29-35).

What a description! But the saddest thing is that our nation's economy is built on these vices. Social drinking is acceptable. And liquor advertisement is used to sponsor everything from college scholarships to professional sports, with the poor being the biggest losers. The tobacco industry is the the sixth-largest industry in this country, with most of its products sold to American citizens. Twenty-nine billion dollars a year is spent on tobacco products by Americans, with a high percentage of the purchasers being the poor. Is there any question why modern economics hasn't been able to deal with the problem of poverty?

Enough about the causes. To know what causes a problem is only half the answer.

Possible Solution to Poverty

In prescribing solutions to poverty, we must keep in mind that poverty will never be completely eradicated in this world. We can only alleviate poverty. All solutions will only be partial ones. The problem of poverty is not man's alone. God also holds Himself responsible for the poor. Therefore, we as human beings need not deal with the problem of poverty alone. This is a joint venture between us and God.

Our Attitude Determines the Attitude of the Poor

There is a serious negative attitude about the poor in America. I see these attitudes whenever welfare is discussed. I hear the nasty comments made when poor people move into a middle-class neighborhood with the help of government assistance. I watch the responses of the affluent when the poor pay for their groceries with food stamps. Even in the churches of America, the poor are not really welcomed.

And then, with these negative attitudes, we the affluent sit down to draw up programs to help the poor. Haven't we learned yet that what we think about people and how we feel about them affects how we treat them and how we design programs to help them?

In the *Harvard Business Review* several years ago, an article appeared on the response of employees to management. It was discovered that, to a large extent, employees responded to management based on what management thought about them and expected from them. In other words, how people respond to us is often affected by our attitudes about them.

As already noted, there is a negative attitude toward the poor in this country. If you are poor, you are often thought to be dirty, lazy, ignorant, uncouth, second-class citizens, and maybe even a little less than human. The poor in this country are treated as if they have some kind of contagious disease.

In human economies, you are somebody because you have something. A man's worth in today's American economy, for example, is based on what he drives, where he lives, what schools he has attended, what degrees he has earned, and even what kind of people he associates with. And since the poor man has none of these, he is thought of as being nothing.

Few really want to be bother with the poor. Many programs—whether those of the government, the church, or a charitable organization—reflect this negative attitude. Help is given to the poor with long-handled serving spoons. We don't want to get close to them. Most programs offer a quick-fix approach. Soup kitchens, government-surplus food distribution, aid to dependent children (ADC), food stamps, and community service centers have their place. But poor people need more than food, clothing, and a place to stay. They are human beings, with three dimensions to their lives that must be addressed in any helping situation.

A positive attitude toward the poor is a must if we are to take seriously the job of helping them. In Theo-Economics, the dignity of all men is foundational. Since all are created in the "image of God," all deserve respect and dignity. That includes the poor. A man's economic condition should not determine the kind of treatment he gets. All men should be treated with dignity and respect.

While I was attending the theological seminary, my wife and I saw some very lean days. On one of those lean days, we decided to go and apply for food stamps. The very air in the welfare office reeked of dehumanizing elements. After waiting over an hour, the social worker called us into her booth. We could almost smell the aroma of superiority emanating from the social worker. Everything about the process reflected the attitude that poor people are nothing. The experience was so humiliating that my wife and I determined never to go back. We decided then and there that we would rather go hungry than to suffer such a loss of dignity again.

An old saying goes, "Beggars can't be choosers." It appears that those who seek to provide help for the poor take this saying to mean that poor people must accept anything that is dished out to them. There is little care in the way poor people are spoken to. They are made to wait long periods of time without any consideration of other things they would like to do or need to do. They are expected to accept the leftovers — worn out and second-hand merchandise — without one word of complaint.

It appears that many people who service the poor have never had to wait in line for food stamps and government handouts. They have never had to be on the receiving end. Therefore they have no sympathy for the poor. In Theo-Economics, we learn that the Golden Rule applies in all our dealings: "Do unto others as you would have them do unto you."

Our attitude does affect how we treat the poor. Attitude determines the kinds of program designed to help the poor as well as the manner in which they are implemented. Check your own attitude right now. How do you feel about the poor? Do you believe all poor people are lazy? Have you convinced yourself that all the poor want to be poor? Do you think poor people are ignorant and incapable of learning?

These questions not only check our attitude about the poor,

but they also strike at one of the major reasons that the war on poverty has not worked in this country. Theo-Economics demands that we look at all people as our brothers and sisters. It mandates that we treat people with dignity, no matter what their economic condition.

Give Self-help, not Self-pity.

The last thing poor people need is pity. The poor are well aware of their condition, so they do not need any more reminders. What the poor need are programs that will teach them how to help themselves. The social programs of this country have almost completely ruined several generations of people. Help given out indiscriminately always does more harm than good.

I have spent years on the front lines of America, ministering to the poor. I have seen what the "free-lunch" program has done to people. Whenever people are not required to put forth any effort to receive help, it teaches them to be dependent. Free-lunch programs destroy human initiative. They encourage selfishness and helplessness. Often they lead to idleness, extravagance, and intemperance.

Theo-Economics teaches that no man who can earn his own livelihood has a right to depend on others. "For even when we were with you, this we commanded you, that if any would not work, neither should he eat" (1 Timothy 3:10). But by the same token, Theo-Economics demands just wages for the laborer. We cannot expect a man to work, when it is more profitable to draw welfare. Theo-Economics encourages the personal responsibility of the poor, but also the corporate responsibility of the nation. We must teach the poor how to help themselves. We must help them to become productive. The old Chinese proverb says, "Give a man a fish and you feed him for a day; teach him how to fish and you feed him for a lifetime."

Every program should give the poor additional tools to help themselves. Helping the poor to become independent should be the goal of every program for the underprivileged. This approach to helping is more difficult, because it calls for more personal effort on the part of people. It takes time, energy, and effort. Few people are willing to make that kind of sacrifice. It is much easier to give away food, clothes, and even money. Once that is done, you can be on your way. But real help for the poor exacts a price.

"Real charity helps men to help themselves. If one comes to our door and asks for food, we should not turn him away hungry. His poverty may be the result of misfortune. But true beneficence means more than mere gifts. It means a genuine interest in the welfare of others. We should seek to understand the needs of the poor and distressed, and to give them the help that will benefit them most. To give thought and time and personal effort costs far more than merely to give money. But it is the truest charity.

"Those who are taught to earn what they receive will more readily learn to make the most of it. And in learning to be self-reliant, they are acquiring that which will not only make them self-sustaining, but will enable them to help others."[2]

Give Property to lift out of Poverty

In Chapter 8, "The American Dream or the American Nightmare?" we will discuss the subject of property at length. So here I will just introduce the topic.

Property is a vital part of any self-help program for those in poverty. Many of America's poor live in crowded, rat-infested housing in the inner city. They spend their lives in asphalt jungles detached from nature. There are many poor people in this country who have never taken a leisurely walk in the woods. Many know little about nature. The crime-ridden, God-forsaken cities of this country breed poverty. We would do the poor a great favor by allowing them to own a few acres of land away from the cities. A little place of their own would spark new life in many of them. It would help them regain dignity lost in the social welfare programs of this country. With proper training, the poor could learn how to support themselves from small gardens and home industries.

I saw on the news some time ago a story about a lady in California who started a rehabilitation program for prisoners. The program was built around garden therapy. After doing research, this lady was convinced that putting inmates to work tilling the soil would soften their characters and teach them valuable lessons of industry, patience, persistence, and hard work.

To stay in the program, inmates are required to work so many hours each week in the gardens. They not only till the soil but plant the seeds and harvest the crops. The crops raised in the gardens are then sold to the public. The profits are then divided among the inmates and the corporation. From all indications, the program has been a smashing success. Many of the inmates learned valuable coping and work skills that have turned them away from a life of crime.

Millions of acres of government-owned land are available for use in this country. Give the poor an opportunity to purchase some of these choice pieces of land at reduced rates. Then, design training programs to teach them the skills necessary for success in their new venture. A program like this would pay dividends far into the future. It would foster family values and independence, help alleviate crime, and ease tax burdens.

Motivation, not Manipulation

What the poor need most are people who believe in them. Many have little or no self-worth. They don't believe in themselves. All their lives, they have experienced failure. Success is beyond their comprehension. People in poverty are just like any other human beings — they need encouragement. They need people who can look beneath their poverty and see their inner potential. People to say, "I believe in you." They need successful people to give them positive words to inflate their mental wings. Words are powerful! Napoleon understood the power of words. He used words to push his army to its victories. Emil Ludwig said of him in the Italian campaign: "Half of what he achieves is achieved by the power of words." Sometimes Napoleon told his ragged, hungry army about the good food and comfortable lodging they would find beyond the mountains; on other occasions he pictured his soldiers returning as heroes to their homes.

Solomon expressed it this way: "A word aptly spoken is like

apples of gold in settings of silver" (Proverbs 25:11). Words of encouragement go a long way to motivate those in poverty. Ultimately, what lifts people out of poverty is their own self-determination. When the poor realize that they can, they will. Motivation is helping people to recognize their inner potential. It is encouraging them to take control of their own destiny. It is inspiring them to take responsibility for their lives.

What I have come to understand about alleviating poverty in this country is that we must accept the powerless, the down-trodden, the economically deprived, as our brothers and sisters. A song in the sixties said, "He ain't heavy, he's my brother."

We need to see the poor as part of the family. Carrying the poor then becomes a privilege, not a burden. Attitudes of superiority vanish when we see the poor as close relatives. We will stop designing programs that simply manipulate the poor.

It appears to me that often we reach out to the poor because of fear. We don't want crime to come into our communities. We want to stop the spread of drugs. We don't want our taxes to keep going up. We don't want the poor to riot. So we offer the poor handouts as a means of keeping them quiet and civil.

Whether consciously or unconsciously, we are manipulating them. Manipulation doesn't change people. It just keeps them quiet, until the next time. By far the best way to help the poor is by motivation. This is the approach Theo-Economics sees as the only viable solution. It is the only one that guards the dignity of the poor. It is the only one that teaches them how to fish so that they can feed themselves for a lifetime. Fighting poverty in this country has to be a group effort. Everyone must get involved.

5

You Can Have Wealth

Amerca is one of the few countries in the world where a person can go from rags to riches. It is a land of opportunity. Thousands still flock to our borders looking for a brighter, more prosperous future. Millions dream of coming to America to make it big.

In two and a quarter centuries, this nation has grown to become the richest nation in the world. Despite the sagging economy, the slowdown in the GNP, and the astronomical debt, we still are the financial nerve center of the world. But how do we account for this affluence as a nation? I can assure you that America's wealth was not by accident or chance. Neither was it solely the result of keen business acumen or skillful planning and execution of those plans.

As much as modern economists would like to take credit for the phenomenal economic growth of this nation, the records reveal a divine force at work in the nation's economy. This "Invisible Hand," mentioned earlier, played a large part in the developing prosperity of our country. Theo-Economics recognizes God's generous involvement in the development of

America. It acknowledges that it is God who gives the power to get wealth.

The Old Testament scriptures describe wealth as a gift of God. God blessed Abraham and made him rich in cattle, in silver, and in gold. The Bible states that, as an evidence of divine favor, God gave David, Solomon, Jehoshaphat, and Hezekiah abundant riches and honor.

Remember the man in Chapter 2 who asked, "Does God really make people wealthy?" Implied in this question is the idea that wealth is evil. In my soon-to-be-released book, *The Money Guilt Trip*, I detail why people feel so guilty about money. But for now, the reality is that many see wealth as evil. Many condemn the wealthy simply because they are wealthy. But the Bible does not condemn the rich man because he is rich. It does not declare the acquisition of wealth to be a sin, nor does it say that money is the root of all evil. What the Bible does condemn is ill-gotten wealth. It denounces the abuse and misuse of wealth.

Wealth Without Wisdom

Theo-Economics is the the only economy that gives a reason for wealth. It is the only system that sees the connection between true wealth and wisdom. Notice that I have qualified the word *wealth* with the adjective *true*. The word *wealth* has to be qualified, because there are two kinds of wealth. There is wealth that comes as a result of hard work, diligence, honesty, and trust in God. That is true wealth.

Then there is wealth gained through close deals, dishonesty, cheating, oppression, and preying on the weaknesses of men. This wealth also comes at the loss of integrity, family, health, friends, and a relationship with God. We call this false wealth. False wealth is wealth without wisdom, reason, or purpose. Human economics can only generate fake wealth.

In contemporary economics, wealth has no real purpose. And where there is no purpose, you cannot expect direction. And where there is no direction, you can expect indulgence, wastefulness, selfishness, and the abuse and misuse of wealth. We see the abuse and misuse of wealth every day in the conspicuous consumption of today's affluent. We even have a hit television show glamorizing purposeless wealth: "Lifestyles of the Rich and Famous." Now, many are having "caviar wishes" and hoping for "champagne dreams."

Purposeless accumulation of wealth has spawned a new, bold generation of people. During the earlier days of this country, people of wealth thought it offensive, unethical, and even sinful to flaunt their wealth. But nowadays, we have the BMW generation. They see nothing wrong with flaunting their wealth. Isn't that the purpose of wealth—to show it off? Or so they think.

The expensive cars, the designer clothes, the fancy shoes, the diamond-studded watches, the well-appointed suburban homes, the exotic vacations, the private health clubs—all are the results of wealth without wisdom. But can we really expect anything different from an economic system that denies the involvement of God in human economy? The denial of God is the death of wisdom. "For the Lord gives wisdom, and from his mouth comes knowledge and understanding" (Proverbs 2:6). When wisdom takes wings and flies away, wealth becomes pretentious and pernicious.

But Theo-Economics harnesses wealth by giving it purpose. Again, wealth is not something that comes to men solely as a result of their personal diligence in business. God is an active player—or should be—in man's accumulation of riches. Therefore, He gives direction and purpose for its use. There are three primary purposes for wealth.

1. To provide for personal needs.
2. To help humanity.
3. To build the new economy of God.

To Provide for Personal Needs

Since we are material being and not angels, we must care for our physical needs. Food, clothing, and shelter are a must. The accumulation of wealth allows us to take care of those needs. Wealth also allows us to move from the level of mere survival to the level of full and complete living. God never intended the greatest of His creation to live on anything less. Survival living is not God's plan. That is why He gives us the power to get wealth.

We need more than just the physical necessities of life. "Man does not live by bread alone" (Matthew 4:4). We need time to think and to create and recreate. Relationships with other human beings are as important to life as is food. But to build relationships takes time. Wealth permits us free time to do those things. Until recent years, men have spent the majority of their days scratching for their daily bread. There was very little, if any, time for relationships or recreation.

Purposeful material wealth offers us a better quality of life. It allows us the ability to enjoy the things that are of lasting value. Things like good health, a happy marriage, time spent with children and friends, wholesome reading, and time alone with God. Money can't buy these. But it does buy us time to develop them if we so choose.

Building wealth with the purpose of providing for our personal needs has still another dimension. Wealth building is never by luck or fortune. Wealth is the result of God rewarding a man's diligence, hard work, persistence, patience, faith, temperance, and integrity. Therefore, a direct by-product of true wealth building is the development of a good character.

I have a friend with whom I have been working for years in the area of his money management. This had been an extremely weak point in his character. In helping him deal with an almost insurmountable financial dilemma, I encouraged him to begin using his talents to make extra money, in order to clear up a huge deficit. After years of prodding and praying, he finally mustered the courage to produce a product he had been sitting on for years.

It took him about two weeks, going almost night and day, to get the product ready for market. Exhausted but encouraged, he took his product to potential clients. In one week of selling, he was able to recoup the full cost of production and turn a profit. In a phone conversation, he confessed, "I have never worked that hard on any project in my life. Just imagine where I'd be now if I had been working this hard all the time!"

In a subsequent phone conversation, he admitted, "While I was selling, I discovered I didn't want to spend my hard-earned money on junk. The thought of wasting money after all my hard labor just didn't sit well with me."

Through wealth building, my friend has learned the lessons of hard work, persistence, patience, courage, thrift, and trust in God. Again and again, as I have taught people how to build wealth the Theo-Economics way, I have seen lives changed for the better. I have watched people start to live what Stephen Covey calls "principle-centered lives." It has been a joy helping people enjoy "the more abundant life."

This is God's purpose in giving us wealth—so that our lives might be fuller and more complete in Him. But in providing for our personal needs, there is no room for personal indulgence.

A recent commercial on television makes me cringe every time I hear it. It says "total indulgence, zero guilt." This commercial plays to the purposeless wealth building that dominates human economy. It drives deep the philosophy already popular in modern economy that a little indulgence is all right.

But in Theo-Economics, indulgence has absolutely no place at all. This mandate is best shown in the New Testament parable of the rich fool. God blessed the rich fool with a bumper crop. After his needs were satisfied, instead of looking for meaningful places to use his wealth, he tore down his old barns and built newer, bigger ones in which to hoard what was left over. It was his intention to indulge himself. But God had something else in mind.

> "You fool! This very night your life will be demanded from you. Then who will get what you have prepared for yourself? This is how it will be with anyone who stores up things for himself but is not rich toward God" (Luke 12:20, 21).

This man was a not bad man. He was just a man content to build wealth according to the principes of a human economic system—a system that taught him that true wealth can be gained without wisdom. In other words, without God. This man is called a fool, not because he didn't have any sense, because it is obvious from the story he had enough sense to become wealthy. But he was called a fool because he denied the existence of God and His involvement in the economy.

The Bible proclaims "The fool has said in his heart, there is no God" (Psalm 14:1; 53:1). This man, like many today, was a practical atheist. He might have believed that there is a God, but he lived his life and ran his business as if God did not exist. That is why we must take into account the next purpose for wealth.

To Help Humanity

The greatest battle you and I must fight is the battle against self. We are selfish by nature. We come into the world crying for attention. We expect the world to orbit around us and our needs. No parent has been exempt from the difficult task of teaching children concern for others. It is not an easy job. That is because selfishness is embedded deep in our hearts. And even after years of personal development, all of us still have to fight to keep the heart weeded of selfishness.

This second purpose for wealth is twofold. First and primary, we are given wealth to help suffering humanity. Jesus' statement, "The poor will always be with you" (Matthew 26:11) did not place a lock on the ability of certain groups to gain wealth but was the statement of a reality brought about by sin. As sickness, death, and suffering will always be with us, so will poverty. There will always be needs to meet. So then, it becomes the responsibility of the rich to answer the needs of the less fortunate. Wealth is given to them to assist in helping humanity.

The want and wretchedness in our world are constant appeals to our compassion and sympathy. The needy in our communities remind us that there is just one human family. Our reaching out to help suffering humanity ties us to the poor with ties that are difficult to break. Of course, there are limits and precautions that we must take as we aid the needy, but that should not hinder our concern or help.

I believe that if the wealthy of this country would take this responsibility seriously, there would be little need for the government to become involved in meeting the needs of the poor.

Millions of wealthy people in this country could be involved in meeting the needs of the underprivileged.

But who are the wealthy in the country? If you missed it earlier, I have been using the term *we*. You and I are the wealthy. It is easy for us to focus on the few billionaires and the thousands of millionaires who live in the United States and tell them what they need to do. And I do believe that the super-rich have greater responsibilities and can do far more than what they are doing. There should be more super-rich like the industrialist Gene Lang, who adopted entire classes from Harlem schools and sent them to college. Or talk-show personality Oprah Winfrey, who has committed her entire earnings from an upcoming movie for the renovation of a low-income housing project in Chicago.

But I must turn my comments to the millions of people like you and me who have good jobs, a good education, and great futures. What are we doing to help the poor? We are part of the wealthy in this nation. We may not have millions in the bank. But look at what we do have. Three-bedroom, two-and-a-half-bathroom houses. Two cars parked inside a two-car garage. Color televisions and telephones in every room. And gadgets of all shapes, sizes, and prices. Affluence fairly oozes from our pores.

Felix Rohatyn, an investment banker, was quoted in *US News & World Report,* saying:

> "I have never seen the kind of money being spent that people are spending today. It is conspicuous consumption without conscience. We have had other periods of this—after a good market in the 1960's we saw some of it—but the lavish amounts spent on co-op apartments and houses in the Hamptons exceed previous eras. Or maybe I'm just getting more sensitive to it. The Concorde is an expensive airplane ride—maybe twice the business-class fare—and I frequently see women who are flying to Paris for fitting of their clothes, and flying back on the next Corcorde."[1]

But we still say we don't have enough to help the poor. The money we spend on fast foods alone would put a big dent in the war against poverty. How many needs could be met with the money we spend on video rentals? Now, I'm not knocking the rental of videos, even though I do think we waste too much productive time and money on a luxury that doesn't pay off.

What I am saying is that we have no excuse for not meeting the needs of suffering humanity. We have a responsibility that is constantly being put off onto the government and the super-rich. Anthony Campolo, in a recent book, challenges the reader with the idea that one person can make a difference.

Mother Teresa thought she could. This one lone lady took on a ministry to the "untouchables" of Calcutta. The "untouchables" are the poor of Calcutta who literally live on the garbage heaps outside the city. No one would help them. But Mother Teresa recognized her wealth, was moved to compassion over the needs of the desperately poor, and decided to make a difference.

We are all called to make a difference. We must fight against the "rugged individualism" idea of contemporary economics that militates against selflessly venturing to help the down and out. We must become a part of this God-economy that sees every person in need as a neighbor.

The biblical story of the Good Samaritan serves as a model for those of us who accept Theo-Economics. Ellen White, in her book *Christ's Object lessons*, describes it this way:

"In journeying from Jerusalem to Jericho, the traveler had to pass through a portion of the wilderness of Judea. The road led down a wild, rocky ravine, which was infested with robbers, and was often the scene of violence. It was here that the traveler was attacked, stripped of all that was valuable, and left half dead by the wayside. As he lay thus, a priest came that way; he saw the man lying wounded and bruised, weltering in his own blood; but he left him without rendering any assistance. He 'passed by on the other side.' Then a Levite appeared. Curious to know what had happened, he stopped and looked at the sufferer. He was convicted of what he ought to do, but it was not an agreeable duty. He wished that he had not come that way so that he would not have seen the wounded man. He persuaded himself that the case was no concern of his, and he too 'passed by on the other side.'

"But a Samaritan, traveling the same road, saw the sufferer, and he did the work that the others had refused to do. With gentleness and kindness he ministered to the wounded man. 'When he saw him, he had compassion on him and went to him, and bound up his wounds, pouring in oil and wine, and set him on his own beast, and brought him to an inn, and took care of him. And on the morrow when he departed, he took out two pence, and gave them to the host, and said unto him, Take care of him; and whatsoever thou spendest more, when I come again, I will repay thee.'"[2]

As the wealthy of this country, our role is the same as that of the Good Samaritan. We are called to love our neighbor as ourselves. Who is our neighbor? It is every person who needs our help. Our neighbor is every soul who is wounded and bruised by poverty. Our neighbor is everyone who is the property of God. Wealth is a call to responsibility—the responsibility of helping humanity.

But helping humanity carries with it mutual benefits. You cannot give without receiving something in return. The law of nature says, "you reap what you sow." So when we take from our wealth and give to the poor, the blessings return. This is the blessing of true satisfaction. Nothing is more fulfilling than to help someone. Take a moment to remember the feeling you had as you last helped someone in need. Money can't buy that feeling. If you are like me, what I received back in that sense of fulfillment was far more valuable than the help I gave.

I mentioned earlier how selfish we are by nature. It is natural for us to live only for ourselves. One of the biggest industries in this country is that of personal-care products. We enjoy pampering ourselves with colognes, oils, and makeup. Our modern economy caters to our selfishness. Advertisers tell us that we should indulge ourselves.

Albert Hirschman, in an article entitled, "Shifting Involvement," writes:

"The world I am trying to understand in this essay is the one in which men think they want one thing and then, upon getting it, find out to their dismay that they don't want it nearly as much as they thought . . . and that something else, of which they were hardly aware, is what they really want."[3]

Selfishness leads to the accumulation of more and more things. Theo-Economics sees helping humanity as an excellent cure for selfishness. When we reach out beyond ourselves to help the disadvantaged, we starve selfishness. The more we give to help others, the more selfishness is squeezed out of us. It is true that "It is more blessed to give than to receive" (Acts 20:35). As we give from our wealth to help humanity, we simply make an investment in our own happiness.

But wealth doesn't stop with individuals. Look at the churches of America. Religion is a big business. In some communities it is the biggest business. The care of the poor and downtrodden was originally the work of the church. But as government became more involved in meeting the needs of the poor, the church began to step out of the picture.

Of course, there are some churches that are still involved in community service, and I am well aware of the sixties and seventies, when the church became highly involved in what is called the social gospel. But as I view the countryside, the church is not carrying its responsibility as it ought. The church, like society, has turned in on itself. From my own experience as I pastored, I saw that the great majority of my churches' income went to take care of their own needs. To be completely honest, almost all of this income went to meet the churches' needs.

And I know we can give all kinds of rationales for this. But it still doesn't change the fact that the needs of the poor are not being met. I do believe that if local churches across America took it upon themselves to fight poverty in their own cities and communities, there would be no need for food stamps or any other government-sponsored program.

Finally, we have wealthy businesses, both large and small. To be a small business in America is a brave undertaking. The overhead and the competition is great, because most of these businesses operate solely on the principles of a human economy. Larger companies have more capital to work with and are having a better go of it, but they too have seen cuts in their profit margins. But I am convinced that business must do more to fight poverty in this country. Just as they derive their profits from the community, they should find ways to invest back into the community. Of course, many businesses feel overtaxed and are carrying too much of the load already.

But the truth of the matter is that most businesses are not suffering from over-taxation but from too much overhead. Their businesses are suffocating from debt. It has a strangle-hold on their operations. I will talk more about debt in Chapter 9— "The National Addiction."

Studies have shown that there are two major reasons for business failure: under-capitalization, which simply means the owner didn't count the cost before going into business, and poor management. I have a special burden for American businessmen. That is one of the reasons I have written this book. Businessmen have a special place in Theo-Economics.

One of my favorite writers makes this statement about businessmen in the Old Testament:

"The Lord made Daniel and Joseph shrewd managers. He could work through them because they did not live to please their own inclination, but to please God.

"The case of Daniel has a lesson for us. It reveals the fact that a business man is not necessarily a sharp, policy man. He can be instructed by God every step. Daniel, while prime minister of the kingdom of Babylon, was a prophet of God, receiving the light of heavenly inspiration. Worldly, ambitious statesmen are represented in the word of God as grass that groweth up and as the flower of the grass that fadeth. Yet the Lord desires to have in His service intelligent men, men qualified for various lines of work. Businessmen who will weave the grand principles of truth into all their transactions. And their talents should be perfected by most thorough study and training. If men in any line of work need to improve their opportunities to become wise and efficient, it is those who are using their ability in building up the kingdom of God in the world."[4]

I know that some who read this book will feel that it is too religious. They will wonder how business and religion can mix. But what I have come to understand is that unless we start encouraging businessmen to mix religion with their business, as many of our founding fathers did, the poor and our nation will suffer.

Businessmen have a special gift for building wealth. If the businessmen of America would wake up to their responsibility, not only would the needs of the poor be met, but we would experience prosperity in this nation as never before. This is what Theo-Economics is about. It's about releasing wealth potential so that the third and final purpose of wealth can be accomplished.

To Build the New Economy of God

Don't turn me off now! This is where it really gets good. There are many doomsday books on the market. Some paint graphic pictures of the economic condition of America. By the time you finish reading, you wonder if it's even worth living. Then too, we see publications that specialize in doomsday reports about the destruction of our natural resources: global warming; holes in the ozone layer; polluted air, land, and water. What is all this leading to?

Fear!

I do believe that we have a serious crisis both in our economy and in our environment. We need to take immediate steps to stop the destruction of the ozone layer. We need to monitor more carefully the toxic waste from both industry and government. And we do need to get a firm hold on our runaway economy. But fear never helps remedy problems. Fear brings on blindness and paralysis. Have you ever been so scared you couldn't move? That is what happens when we spend time focusing on doomsday. Yes, recognize that we have problems. Discuss them. Debate them. But then spend time looking for answers. Theo-Economics does just that. It focuses all of its energy on solutions.

Our national problems are extremely complicated. And the only real answer is for a complete reorganizing of things. To fix the pollution problem, we need a new earth. To fix the economy, we need a new economy. This much-needed reorganization is a part of this new economy. Theo-Economics has as its foundational purpose the building up of the kingdom of

God—a kingdom where cooperation takes the place of competition. A kingdom where there is no more sickness, death, or poverty. A kingdom where everybody is somebody.

Those who enter into the economy of God want to build up that kingdom. So a large portion of their wealth goes to build it. They realize that each dollar invested in a local Christian church or gospel mission that teaches the Word of God helps to build that kingdom on earth.

Yet instead of building true wealth, in recent years modern economists, in an attempt to revamp the old human economy, have sought to make economics a pure science. They have designed mathematical computations to verify and develop economic theories in their attempt to make economics totally scientific. These mathematical computations are supposed to help produce wealth—or at the least predict the loss of wealth.

But econometrics—the science of economy—has failed to produce the desired effect. What these economists seem to forget is that economics is not a science but a philosophy. Human economy is built on false philosophies, so it cannot stand. On the other hand, Theo-Economics is built on the solid foundation of the laws of God. The Ten Commandments, as given in God's Word, govern the economic theories of Theo-Economics. These laws, which become also a philosophy of life, when obeyed, assure prosperity for a nation.

Moses, in giving instruction to the nation of Israel, said:

> "If you fully obey the Lord your God and carefully follow all his commands I give you today, the Lord your God will set you high above all the nations of the earth" (Deuteronomy 28:1).

Those same words hold true for any nation that desires prosperity. Again, wealth is not something we create. It is God who gives us the power to get wealth. The moral law of God is summed up in these words:

> "Love the Lord your God with all your heart and with all your soul and with all your mind. This is the first and great commandment. And the second is like it. Love your neighbor as yourself" (Matthew 22:37-39).

Our founding fathers were convinced of the need for the

moral law of God. They were persuaded that the prosperity of the nation was dependent on adherence to the laws of God.

The Dangers of Wealth

But we cannot leave the subject of wealth without dealing with its dangers. Modern economists have no way of dealing with this issue, because ethics is not a part of their discussion. But let it be known that there are dangers that come along with wealth. Theo-Economics sounds the alarm. A need exists to protect a nation and its people from the dangers that come with affluence. I see four of these dangers, summarized by the following acronym:

S-I-N-S

Self-sufficiency. The foremost danger in wealth building is that of self-sufficiency. The disease "me-itis" sets in. And we come to believe that we really accumulated our wealth all by ourselves. In America, we have a special place in our hearts for a self-made man. Again, this is part of that "rugged individualism" concept that has helped ruin this country.

Many of us today are like Nebuchadnezzar, in the Old Testament book of Daniel. We look out over this great nation and come to the false conclusion that we built it—that it was our own blood, sweat, and tears that brought us to where we are today. What a sad conclusion! If God hadn't been on our side, we wouldn't be the nation we are today. We wouldn't have the individual wealth so many of us have. Modern economists don't seem to know that our national and personal wealth came "Not by might, nor by power, but by my Spirit says the Lord" (Zechariah 4:6). They seem to believe—and many other Americans along with them—that it was their computations and theories that created wealth for this nation. Wrong! God did it! We were just players on His stage as He directed and orchestrated everything to His final end.

This attitude of self-sufficiency has produced a generation that has turned its back on God. Businessmen seldom take God into their work. Economists talk about business cycles, but never about God's intervention. But it is this same self-sufficiency that is the cause of men shaking in their boots as they look at our messed-up economy. They have no answers.

Indulgence. History records that every nation of antiquity began its downward spiral to defeat and destruction when its citizens gave way to indulgent lifestyles. Historically, the cycle is this: Affluence permits leisure time. Leisure time, misused, creates idle time. Idle time leads to indulgence, which leads to moral decay and destruction. Our country is experiencing economic anemia because of our long years of indulgence. Because of the indulgence of appetite, we have not only overweight adults but overweight, out-of-shape children. Every day, we are literally eating away our wealth.

The lifeblood of our working force is also being sucked dry through the indulgence of sex. We find it easy to protest the lifestyle of gays and lesbians, which is offensive to me too, but what about the growing number of sexually active teenagers? What about the even larger group of adults who practice sex outside of marriage? Studies have shown that sex outside of marriage places a drain on a person's life force.

Finally, look at how Americans waste millions of dollars and hundreds of potentially productive hours worshiping at the temple of professional sports. Now don't get me wrong—I like sports. But don't you think that we have over-indulged ourselves as a nation, when recreation has become a major industry in this country?

Neglect. The natural consequence of indulgence is the neglect of the poor and underprivileged. Indulgence focuses on self. And when self is the center of national life, others do not count. We become blind to the needs of others. In the richest nation in the world, there is no excuse for thirty million people being without healthcare. In this prosperous nation, there is no reason for children to go to bed hungry. In this affluent country, there is no rationale that can be provided for the fact that millions of young people have no opportunity for higher education.

Superiority. I touched on this a little in the previous chapter on poverty, but let me expand further now. There is a certain amount of arrogance that comes with wealth. You don't have to be humble when you have the power of money.

One day a man was dining in an unfamiliar restaurant. After a long wait, the waitress finally came to take his order.

"What do you want?" the waitress snapped.

"I would like mashed potatoes, gravy, the vegetable of today, and a steak, well done," the gentlemen replied as calmly as he could.

She took the order, and without saying another word, left. A half hour passed, and the man had not received his order. So he called for the manager. When the manager came, he was just as rough and indifferent as the waitress.

The gentlemen said to himself, "I don't have to take this." Then, without saying a word, he abruptly left the table, went to the pay phone, and made a call.

After a few minutes, he returned. He called for the manager and the waitress.

"You are fired!" the gentlemen told them. "You won't treat me like that again." His phone call had resulted in the purchase of the restaurant.

Wealth is power. If we aren't careful, this power has a tendency to produce arrogance, impatience, and the feeling that we are better than others. I see it all the time in middle-class America. Many feel that because of where they live, what they drive, where they work, and who they know, that they are better than those less fortunate. You see them looking down their noses. You hear this superior attitude coming through in expressions like, "We don't want those kind of people in our neighborhood," or, "I don't want my kids hanging around those people."

But time is the great equalizer. You see, all of us, in time, will get sick and need some help. Then, these same poor people will have to take care of you in the hospital. I had a boss who used to say to all his male employees, "Men, be careful how you treat your wife—she may have to change your diapers one day."

Russell Conwell, a nineteenth-century preacher and educator, became well known for his speech, "Acres of Diamonds." This speech motivated thousands to search for wealth right in their own backyard. But Conwell's speech did not merely exhort self-help, but pointed toward a duty to get rich.

"Opportunity lurks in everyone's backyard," said Conwell. "Everyone should get rich." But Conwell was the perfect example of someone concerned with true wealth. He delivered "Acres of Diamonds" more than six thousand times to admiring audiences, and earned from it $8 million in an age when a soda and a sandwich cost five cents.

Conwell believed that one should get rich not merely to be rich, but to help others. So he took the $8 million and founded Temple University. That is the message of Theo-Economics. God places in our hearts the desire to acquire wealth, not to indulge ourselves, but to provide for personal needs, to help humanity, and to build up the kingdom of God.

A Message to our Government

To you, our divinely ordained government, now is the time to recognize again where this nation's wealth has come from—God. You must stop the waste, indulgence, and neglect, if this nation is to once again be the force for good God ordained it to be. No nation that neglects the mandates of God can expect to continue prospering. But any nation that turns back to the claims of God will experience His generous hand.

A Message to Every Citizen

You are the basis of this nation's wealth. What you do with the money you have will determine the destiny of the nation. The government does not produce money—you do! So you must take responsibility for how this nation's wealth is used. You must manage wisely the wealth you have. Remember that wealth building is in your hands.

I believe that every citizen in this country has the ability to produce wealth. Go out and find the "Acres of Diamonds" in your own backyard. But never forget that "It is God that gives us the power to get wealth" (Deuteronomy 8:18).

6

The Job You Will Never Lose

International Harvester, the big truck, tractor, and heavy equipment manufacturer, had a sign over its main gate at the old Memphis plant years ago that said, "International Harvester Forever." And for over three decades, men and women worked at this large plant with a great sense of security. In fact, people liked working for the company because it had such a great reputation. Fair treatment of employees, high wages, excellent benefits, good working conditions — what more could an employee ask for?

Many came to believe the sign, "International Harvester Forever." Fathers told their sons, "Get a high school diploma, and there will be a job waiting for you at International Harvester." And to a large extent, that was true. There were always jobs available at International Harvester, because it was such a large plant involved in a big business. No one ever dreamed that International Harvester would close its doors in Memphis. One

75

generation of men had already retired from the company, and a new generation had put in as much as fifteen years. Working at International Harvester appeared to be "the job you would never lose."

Then the bottom dropped out of the economy. International Harvester started having financial troubles. In an effort to save the company, it began to shut down plants all over the country. Still no one ever dreamed that the Memphis plant would close. It was a major plant for this international company.

But in the earlier eighties, International Harvester closed its Memphis doors. Forever was true. But thousands of employees had believed that "forever" applied to jobs. Instead, it applied to the closing of the doors at the Memphis plant.

How would you feel if all your hopes, dreams, and your lifelong career went up in smoke when the company you worked for went belly up?

A couple of years later, in that same city, a chain of grocery stores owned by a long-time resident starting having financial problems. The employees were never made aware of the financial troubles. They believed, as did most people in those days, that if you got a good job, worked hard, were honest, were never late, went the extra mile, and acted right, you had a job for as long as you wanted it. But they were sadly mistaken.

Christmas Eve of 1982, the owners closed down all their stores for the holidays, never to open again. They had gone out of business and had not even given their employees any prior warning or notification.

What would you feel like if you went back to your job after the Christmas holidays and were greeted with the sign "We've Gone Out Of Business"?

When we talk about unemployment in this country, what we see is facts, not faces. We think of plants, not people. We hear numbers, not names. But unemployment is about people — real people. People who could very well be your next-door neighbors. They could be relatives or friends. Or — maybe even you.

But no matter who it strikes, unemployment is devastating.

In recent years, millions have experienced the loss of a job. From white collar to no collar. From college professors to high school dropouts. From corporate executives to motel maids. The human wreckage is enormous. Some three million employable people currently walk the streets of America, hoping, wishing, even begging for work. What kind of answer can we give them? Is there any hope for the unemployed?

Theo-Economics says, "Yes!" There is hope for people out of work. There is an answer to unemployment. The answer to joblessness in Theo-Economics is grounded in the concept that man is created in the "image of God" — that every human being has divine attributes — that there is an "Invisible Hand" showing concern for and involved in the care and protection of each citizen.

Theo-Economics begins the discussion of unemployment with an understanding of work. Work was given by God for the benefit of man. From the very beginning, our first parents were given the job of dressing the garden. God gave employment to the original pair to show the sanctity of work. Work is not a necessary evil, but a purposeful activity. It is activity ordained by God for our welfare. It is one of God's chosen methods of character development.

John Murray, in his book, *Principles of Conduct*, writes extensively about the "Ordinance of Labor." He sees work as a divine mandate — as an integral part of man's life. He states:

> "'The Lord God put Adam in the garden of Eden to dress it and to keep it' (Genesis 2:15). Here is explicit allusion to Adam's specific employment, and we must recognize that such labor is not a curse but a blessing. It finds its ground and sanction in the fact that man's life is patterned after the divine example established in the creation and formation of the universe, which constitutes the realm of man's existence and activity.

> "That Adam's labor consisted in dressing the garden and keeping it informs us that it was highly worthy of man's dignity as created after the divine image to be employed in so mundane a task. This is eloquent warning against the impiety of despising and judging unworthy of our dignity the tasks which we call menial. And one cannot but suspect that the widespread tendency to take flight from agricultural and related

pursuits springs from an underestimation of the dignity of manual toil and often times reflects an unwholesome ambition which is the fruit of impiety. There is warrant for the judgment that economics, culture, morality, and piety have suffered grave havoc by failure to appreciate the nobility of manual labor."[1]

But work, in contemporary society, has boiled down to a paycheck. It has become a meaningless activity that adds to the stress and strain of life. Millions of Americans dread going to work. Work is not about fulfillment and accomplishment but production and profits. In many jobs today, employees are encouraged to leave their brains at home. So while millions are unemployed, millions more hate their jobs, only keeping them because they must pay their bills. Added to the meaningless work is the frustration of being busy but not really working.

While in the seminary, I took a job as a "building engineer" (janitor). My job was to clean two bathrooms and keep a hallway waxed and buffed. I was given two hours to do a job that took an hour at the most to complete.

Having grown up in America, I was well aware of the "be busy" mentality. To keep from becoming totally bored and brain dead yet stay busy, I rigged a contraption around my neck so I could read a page or two while buffing the floor. I guess one of the secretaries didn't like the idea that I was studying while I worked, so she told my boss. The next day at work I was confronted by an irate boss.

"I hear you're studying on the job!" he shouted.

"Sir, I haven't been studying—just reading while working," I replied as calmly as possible.

"You can't do both—it's impossible," he chided.

"Sir, have you had any complaints about my work?" I answered, trying now to reason with him.

"No, but that doesn't matter. You're not supposed to study on the job!" he shouted in an intimidating voice.

By this time I was thoroughly frustrated and angry, and I shouted, "I guess all you want is for me to look busy!"

"That's right—you need to look like you're working."

I left that job the same day. I never could buy into a philosophy more concerned with looking busy than with the results of work. This "be busy" mentality has distorted the true meaning of work. People have learned the art of piddling. They know how to shuffle paper, carry a wrench, even get their hands dirty—all to give the impression of work, while accomplishing little if anything.

This kind of work has little productive value. Many know little of the meaning of real work. In this "make-work" economy, many are denied the satisfaction of fruitful labor and personal fulfillment. The work concept is distorted further by work-aholism. In this modern economy, especially in this western culture, the philosophy of never-ending work prevails. The picture of a successful person is of one who puts in long hours at the office and comes home with a briefcase full of papers to work until midnight.

In the scramble of workers these days to get ahead, it seems that our economists have let slip from their notice the law of diminishing returns. Many seem to have forgotten that after a certain point, work becomes unproductive. They seem to miss the point that efficient, effective, and ethical economics must be concerned more with people than with profits.

People, unlike machines, are designed by their Creator to work six days and rest one. The medical profession verifies that a person needs an average of eight hours of sleep per night and one day a week off for rest. Rest, then, is a vital part of a productive, healthy economy. Theo-Economics not only understands the importance of rest but accepts it as one of God's laws for a prosperous economy.

In the midst of the Ten Commandments, we discover the economic law of rest and labor.

> "Remember the sabbath day by keeping it holy. Six days you shall labor and do all your work, but the seventh day is the sabbath to the Lord your God. On it you shall not do any work, neither you, nor your son or daughter, nor your manservant or maidservant, nor your animals, nor the alien within your gates. For in six days the Lord made the heavens and the earth, the sea, and all that is in them, but he rested on the seventh day. Therefore the Lord blessed the Sabbath day and made it holy" (Exodus 20:8-12).

Theo-Economics views this law as describing God's prosperity cycle. Work six—off one! Work six—off one! Work, work, work, work, work, work—then rest.

John Murray writes:

> "The stress laid upon the six days of labor needs to be duly appreciated. The divine ordinance is not simply that of labor; it is labor with a certain constancy. There is indeed respite from labor, the respite of one whole day every recurring seventh day. The cycle of respite is provided for, but there is also the cycle of labor. And the cycle of labor is as irreversible as the cycle of rest. The law of God cannot be violated with impunity. We can be quite certain that a great many of our physical and economic ills proceed from failure to observe the weekly day of rest."[2]

I learned to swim when I was a freshman in college. Before then, like many, I just played in the water. In the swimming class, my instructor taught us how to swim laps. We came to understand that the test of a real swimmer is his ability to swim laps. In fact, part of the requirement for completing the class was swimming a mile in twenty minutes. That added up to thirty-six laps—or seventy-two lengths of an Olympic-sized pool.

I discovered the trick to doing laps—setting up a rhythm. Stoke, stroke, stroke—breath. Stoke, stroke, stroke—breath. With a rhythm, I could swim many laps before getting tired. God's prosperity cycle becomes man's success cadence.

1. Work.
2. Work.
3. Work.
4. Work.
5. Work.
6. Work.
7. Rest.

God instituted the spiritual and economic law of rest—the Sabbath—for three reasons:

As a Reminder of God's Ownership of the World

First, God's design and desire has always been for man to

prosper and live in a prosperous state. God takes no delight in seeing His creatures suffer and live in poverty. He planned for us to prosper. But in the planning, He made provision to keep before us the true source of all wealth.

As mentioned earlier, there are dangers in prosperity, and the major danger is self-sufficiency. We have a tendency to forget the source of true prosperity. This Sabbath law is a weekly reminder of God's creative power. It is a constant reminder that He is the owner of all things. This rest day becomes God's weekly reminder that "It is God who gives us the power to produce wealth" (Deuteronomy 8:18).

Ellen White, in her book, *The Cosmic Conflict*, writes:

> "The importance of the Sabbath as the memorial of creation is that it keeps ever present the true reason why worship is due to God — because He is the Creator, and we are His creatures . . . It was to keep this truth ever before the minds of men, that God instituted the Sabbath in Eden, and so long as the fact that He is our Creator continues to be a reason why we should worship Him, so long the Sabbath will continue as its sign and memorial. Had the Sabbath been universally kept, man's thoughts and affections would have been led to the Creator as the object of reverence and worship, and there would never have been an idolater, an atheist, or an infidel."[3]

For Improved Physical Health

There are therapeutic benefits in enjoying the rest of the Sabbath. The Hebrew meaning for the word *Sabbath* is "rest." Rest is extremely vital for proper health. The body is somewhat like a storage battery that must be regenerated and recharged. Scientists have proven that rest does allow the body to rebuild and recharge. Even general observation confirms that man accomplishes more in six days with one day off than in seven days without rest.

In the book *Christian Economics*, John R. Richardson gives this persuasive account of how health and production is increased when the Sabbath law is obeyed.

> "During the early days of World War II, there was a tremendous demand for duck, the heavy cloth used for the manufac-

ture of uniforms, tents, and other items necessary in the conduct of warfare. The textile mills immediately converted their machines to produce the material. A Christian was at that time connected with four of these mills, and later five. One of his superiors called him to assign an almost impossible quota. A conversation, like the following, occurred:

"'Of course, we expect you to run the mills twenty-four hours a day seven days a week.'

"'I will run the mills twenty-four hours a day, six days a week, but I am not going to run going to run these on Sunday.'

"'Now, every one is running seven days a week; you've got to. The government has said that everybody must run seven days a week.'

"'The government wants that number of yards produced each week. Neither the government nor anybody else is going to make me operate on the Lord's Day.'

"'You can't possibly produce your quota without running on Sundays.'

"'I'll produce that quota running six days a week.'

"As far as we know, these mills are the only ones in the nation that fully met, and usually over-produced, their quota consistently during all the years of the war. They were never open on Sunday."[4]

This kind of miraculous occurrence cannot be explained by modern economic calculations. That's because it is inexplicable. This kind of occurrence is the direct result of "The Invisible Hand" of God rewarding obedience to the Sabbath law of rest.

Mental Benefits

Mental benefits are also derived from this one-day sabbatical. As the body needs refreshment by rest, so does the mind. A change of scenery, a change of conversation, a change from the problem and troubles of work are needed to keep the mind alert and creative. We have all met a person whose conversation is the same all the time. It bores you to death. What you say to the person is, "Take a break! Let's talk about something else." So Sabbath becomes man's "mind break."

I had a friend who was an alcoholic, even though he would never admit it. From time to time he would stop by my house to talk. We would talk for a while; then he would mentally start moving to his longed-for weekend.

"Preacher," he would say, "you don't know what the fast lane is all about, do you?"

"No, I can't say that I do," I would respond.

"Well, I live in the fast lane, and every so often I have to take a mind break. After that, I'm all right."

Well, my friend's idea of a mind break was not what God had in mind when He instituted the Sabbath. My friend's idea of a mind break was going off alone on the weekend and getting sloppy drunk. What's astonishing is that many American workers spend their weekends doing just that. Perhaps the reason some take that kind of "mind break" is because of their uninteresting, nonproductive, brainless jobs. But the "mind break" Theo-Economics calls us to is the Sabbath, that allows us to rest our minds in God. It is a time to reflect on our blessings—a time to unwind.

The Sabbath a Call to Full Employment

The Sabbath rest establishes work as well as rest. This law teaches that man finds fulfillment in work and that there cannot be true Sabbath rest without work. In fact, the Sabbath is a call to full employment. By calling man to this divine rest, God obligates Himself to give man employment.

Adam and Eve, the original pair, were given jobs. They were required to manage the Edenic garden and take care of the animals. God's provision of work for all mankind is seen in His distribution of talents and abilities. Every person comes from the Maker's hand with a special assignment. Some have the ability to teach. Some are good with their hands. Some are good in research. Some have the gift of leadership. Large numbers of people are called to be support personnel.

But no matter what the calling or job, everyone is important. The human family is like the human body, the Bible says. There are many different organs, but just one body. All of the organs of the body are important. The toe may not be a major player in body activity, but it is important for the smooth operation of the body.

In the human family, especially in the context of Theo-Economics, every person is important to the efficient, effective working of the economy. The janitor is as important to the economy as is the Harvard engineer. Unlike human economic systems, that place greater value on particular jobs and persons, Theo-Economics places high value on everyone. This is where the superiority of Theo-Economics shines, for it sees that unemployment can only be solved through the development of human potential—not through industry alone.

It is not industries or businesses that produce but the people behind those entities. Our country has invested hundreds of billions in brick and mortar, dies and tools, gadgets and gizmos. But how much has been spent in developing human potential? How much has been spent to teach proper work ethics? How much has been contributed to motivate the masses of people to reach their personal potential?

Theo-Economics is about empowering people. It endeavors to show that all people must take responsibility for their lives. Every one must be more than just a consumer. For too long, our modern economy has been satisfied with the elite creating the jobs and being responsible for production. But if our nation is to survive, we must do as Theo-Economics recommends—we must empower the masses.

We must make them producers, show them how to become efficient workers, encourage them to develop their talents and abilities, tell them that they can create jobs, and give them the responsibility of helping this nation lift itself out of the pits of financial despair. Theo-Economics lays this responsibility squarely on the shoulders of each individual citizen.

How is this done? In my soon-to-be-released book, *Turn Your Talent Into Cash — the Moral Way to Make Money*, I detail how people can discover their hidden talents and become productive citizens. But for now, I do believe that God has given every person gifts and talents.

Writes John Murray:

"The institution of labor underlies the whole question of human vocation . . . What path of life each individual is to follow in reference to this basic interest of life is to be determined by the proper gift which God has bestowed, and this is the index to the divine will and therefore to the divine call. In connection with the specific kind of labor in which each person is to engage we find this same kind of sanction. Each person's labor is a divine vocation."[5]

Murray makes the point that every man, woman, boy, and girl is endowed by God with natural abilities. I believe that these natural gifts, when developed and put into the marketplace, can produce wealth for both the nation and for individuals.

What disturbs me, in this whole discussion of unemployment, is that it appears that we are talking about dependent children. And if not children, then people who cannot help themselves. But the facts are that most of the people out of work are healthy, able-bodied people.

Now, don't jump ahead of me. I will not go down the same street as the "rugged individualist," who thinks everybody ought to pick themselves up by their own bootstraps. What I am saying is that Theo-Economics is a call to responsibility. No one is allowed to shift the responsibility of his or her life to anyone else, and that includes the unemployed.

There are no guaranteed jobs. No business owes its employees a lifetime of employment. Full lifetime employment is the work of God. When He created us, He committed Himself to our lifetime care. Natural abilities are God's tangible assurance of meeting our needs. I have come to believe that we need to help the unemployed wake up to their natural abilities. They need to be encouraged to develop and invest their talents and then shown how to put their talents into the marketplace. Then they will see that their talents will create "The Job They Can Never Lose."

Unemployment does not mean inability. I was in a resale shop with my wife not too long ago, and to keep myself from being bored, I started talking to the owner. She was a vivacious lady who seemed to have had all the breaks. But I found out that she had never known what it meant to be truly unemployed. Our conversation went something like this:

"How did you get into this kind of business?"

"Well, one day I found myself unemployed—a single parent with two children to support—so I had to do something. Instead of sitting around feeling sorry for myself, I starting thinking about things I had always wanted to do in life. I realized that I had always wanted to own a dress shop."

"But what made you think you could succeed with a dress shop?" I asked.

"Well, I knew I liked sales and had done well in sales at the job I lost. I definitely like clothes, and I felt God was leading me."

"Was it easy getting started?"

"Are you kidding? If I didn't believe in my talents and God, I would never have even tried. You see, I didn't have any money. I did not have any connections, and I am a woman. Those obstacles alone were enough to keep me from making it."

"Looking back," I asked, "how do you feel about losing your job?"

"That was probably the best thing that could have happened to me. I was able to develop my talents and take responsibility for my life, and now I have more freedom and happiness than I could ever ask for."

"What are your plans for the future?" I continued.

"Well, business has been so good that I've decided to open up a children's resale store. There aren't many around. I know I can do well."

This lady's story is not to get you excited about going out and starting your own business, but it's about recognizing your talents and gifts. It's about trusting God to help you develop and use those talents to produce wealth for others and for yourself. This is what the unemployed need to hear.

I have a ninety-three-year-old African-American lady friend who, along with her husband, raised seven children during the depression.

"Tell me about the soup lines," I invited her one day.

"I don't know anything about that," she replied. "There were many unemployed, but my husband and I trusted the Lord and used our talents to make it. My husband had a little moving business and also peddled fresh vegetables. In fact, we bought and paid for a new truck during those dark days."

By the way, my friend never worked outside of the home, and they sent their children to private schools. They were not rich. They just took responsibility for their lives.

Nature informs us that when a pond is stagnant, it dies. When a nation does not maximize its human potential, when it produces "busy lazy people," and when a spirit of apathy and indolence pervades the land, the economy—like the stagnant pond—will dry up and die. People are the lifeblood of this country. We must bring people—all kinds of people—into the discussion of unemployment. Unemployment then becomes everybody's problem, not just that of the ivory-tower economist and the omniscient government.

Theo-Economics calls for responsibility at all levels. It refuses to allow the government or the people constantly to shift the blame and responsibility to others. Theo-Economics outlines the responsibility of the unemployed, of the community, and of the government. ⇨ ⇨ ⇨ ⇨ ⇨ ⇨ ⇨ ⇨

A Message to the Unemployed: SQUAWK

You the unemployed have some choices to make. You can sit on your "pit pot" and pine away until you are blue in the face. That won't change things. It will just make them worse. Or—you can start SQUAWK-ing:

S—**Start** living your life for yourself. Don't allow people, situations, or circumstances to dictate how life will treat you. Take charge of your life. Start using your brain. Look around you and inside you—see the potential. Start looking for those "Acres of Diamonds" in your own backyard.

Q—**Quit** blaming others for your unemployment. Blaming others hurts nobody else but harms you. You might have been done wrong. So what! That won't be the last time, I can assure you. As someone has said, "When you accept the blame, you win the game." You will win because you are taking responsibility for your own destiny. Realize that "The Job You Will Never Lose" is the job you create or keep with your own talents.

U—**Utilize** your abilities. They help to shape your attitude. Take time to learn your abilities. Learn what you are good at. Then cultivate your abilities. If you have leadership abilities, learn all you can about leadership. Then start practicing leadership. If you are good at carpentry, develop that. Again, "The Job You Will Never Lose" is the one where your talents and abilities are used to the fullest.

A—**Attitude** really does determine your altitude. You go only where you believe you can go. Change your attitude. Instead of looking at your unemployment as the worst thing that could have ever happened to you, look at it as an opportunity to grow and learn. Determine that you going to make the best out of a bad situation.

W—**Work** is an important concept. Few people understand the importance of hard, efficient work. This is the time to check your work habits. Are you an on-time person? Do you give 100 percent when you on the job? Are you learning new things on your job so that you can take over when someone isn't there?

But work entails more. Learning how to use your brain is as important as using your brawn—your muscles. Learn how to work not only hard but smart. Then work to find a new job. Put in eight hours a day looking for a job. If you can't find a job, make one.

K—**Keep** your chin up. Keep learning. Keep believing. Use this time to retool, retrain, rethink, and above all, to rebound.

A Message to the Community: CONCERN

What we need to see more of is community involvement in the problem of unemployment. There is no substitute for people helping people. We use community-based programs to deal with crime in our neighborhoods—why not use this same approach with the unemployed? C-O-N-C-E-R-N is an acronym that spells out our community responsibility.

C—**Communication** between neighbors should be encouraged. When someone loses a job, everyone should feel the loss. Help can only come when the problem is known.

O—**Organize** so that the community can know what jobs are available. Organize a community-based skills and ability bank. Organize support groups and relief efforts. Organize to help in retooling and retraining and to teach how to draw unemployment.

N—**Notify** people in other communities about the needs in your own.

C—**Contact** businesses to encourage them to establish themselves in your community. Contact newspapers and other advertising media for help.

E—**Educate** on how to get a job, keep a job, and even create a job.

R—**Remind** people of their importance. Remind them that they can make it.

N—**Never** give up until all are employed in your community who want to be employed.

A *Message to the Government: LOVE*

I know that the government is not often thought of as an entity that loves, but the acronym L-O-V-E gives the government that responsibility.

L—Legislate. The government should continue to write legislation that protects its citizens from oppression. It should use the courts of our land to keep the freedoms that are important to a prosperous economy and that allow people to reach their fullest potential.

O—Officiate. The government also has the responsibility of enforcing the laws of the land that keep oppressive forces at bay.

V—Vacate. The government has never been a good creator of jobs. There are jobs that must be done in the government, but job creation to stimulate the economy is counter-productive. Government stimulation of the economy is like the effect of artificial stimulants on the body. Artificial stimulants work for a while, but in the long run, they end up destroying health.

E—Evaluate. The government should keep tabs on how the overall economy is doing and keep the nation informed. This information should be shared with the general populace to help in personal as well as corporate decisions about unemployment.

Unemployment is a difficult subject. The answer to the problem will never come easy, and there will always be those who will be unemployed. Some people don't want to work. Theo-Economics gives people that right. But just as people have the right not to work, they also have the right to suffer the consequences of their decision. Theo-Economics is compassionate, but it is fair and tough. Paul says, "If you don't work, you don't eat" (see 2 Timothy 3:10).

7

The High Cost of Ignorance

We have at our disposal more information than any generation in the history of the world. Our children are growing up with computers, fax machines, videos, cable television, and soon fiber optics that will allow unlimited information to be available to students and parents at the touch of a keyboard. Yet what has it done for the children?

This is one of the paradoxes of our age.

Our children have mastered video games, but many of them test low in what used to be known as "the three R's": Reading, 'Riting, and 'Rithmatic. America's school children are lagging behind in these crucial subjects, and few seem to be overly concerned. Politicians, parents, and even whole parishes from time to time squawk about the educational system. But most of it is just lip service.

Our nation has apparently moved away from education. It appears no longer to understand the value of learning. Therefore, we are allowing generations of young people to grow up functionally illiterate. Yes, millions are receiving high school diplomas and college degrees of all kinds who are not prepared to face today's world. It's a sad fact that affluence has sapped the brain power of America.

Again a paradox, it would seem that with all the labor-saving devices our young people have that leave them with more time on their hands, they would be studying and reading more. But are they? Not according to what teachers and parents are telling us.

In the early days of America, children had to help with the farm chores. There wasn't much time left for long hours of study. But study they did. Many would snatch an hour here and an hour there, because time was precious. Now, I am not encouraging us to turn back the clock, because there is no such thing as the "good old days." As I listen to the old timers, they don't glamorize those days.

But what I am saying is that we must, as a nation, wake up to the brain drain happening before our eyes. We must see that our nation's economy, as well as its safety, is dependent on the education of its people, both young and old.

Theo-Economics brings us back to our roots. People built this nation. People are the most important commodity in any society. Theo-Economics understands that and shouts loudly that "people must come before profits." It declares that the basis of a sound economy is an educated labor force.

But modern economists apparently don't understand this simple, yet profound truth. They spend precious time working out mathematical formulas that allow them to write harebrained theories that fill up thousands of sheets of paper— that sound good but have little meaningful significance. In fact, of the many books I have read on economics, I haven't found one that deals seriously with education. Many never even mention education as a factor in the economic equation. But Theo-Economics sees education as the foundation of a sound economy.

In the Hebrew economy, parents were required to educate their children.

"Hear, O Israel: the Lord our God, the Lord is one. Love your God with all your heart and with all your soul and with all your strength. These commandments that I give you today are to be upon your hearts. Impress them on your children. Talk about them when you sit at home and when you walk along the road, when you lie down and when you get up. Tie them as symbols on your hands and bind them on your foreheads. Write them on the door frames of your houses and your gates" (Deuteronomy 6:4-7).

The moral law of God formed the basis for Israel's educational system. It was so vital to the nation that all possible time was taken to educate the youth. All the energy of the nation found its focal point in education. That is because man is a creature of thought. Thoughts are the result of ideas gained through education of one kind or another. What a nation feeds the brains of its people will dictate what that nation will become.

In recent years, I entered the teaching profession. This has given me an opportunity to see teaching from the inside. But like so many outsiders, I appreciated teachers before, but didn't give much thought to their real value to society and the economic process.

I should have known better, since I grew up in a teacher's home. My mother was one of those old-time committed teachers — but that was Mom. Until recently, I thought, like the average citizen, "Teachers are a dime a dozen." It was a nice job for those who were not looking to go anywhere in life. But now as I stand before young people on a daily basis, I tremble sometimes at the awesome responsibility of the job. This thought grips me: "In my hands are the minds of a generation of young people."

I wonder sometimes how much we as a nation wrestle with that awesome thought. I do believe that if we thought more about who is teaching our children, there would be a serious ripple effect for good felt in American education.

Competition has wreaked havoc on both the economy and education. The idea of being "number one" has filtered through to just about every area of national life. "It's a dog-eat-dog world" is the competitive reply of millions caught up in the survival of the fittest. At the root of competition is that very anti-biblical concept—the survival of the fittest.

The concept of competition is really just another aspect of the theory of evolution. Evolution teaches that living things (and that includes man) increase in number far more rapidly than is realized. In fact, living things reproduce in numbers so great that earth cannot provide room and food for all their abundant offspring. Men, as well as other animals, must therefore compete with each other for a chance to live.

In this competitive world, any helpful variation gives its owner an advantage over neighbors that are not so well adapted. There is no room in this system for concern for one's neighbor. The only concern is survival. Individuals with greater strength and talents therefore win the struggle for existence. The weak, well—who cares? That's the law of the jungle. "Only the strong survive." Or so says the anti-biblical concept of competition.

This concept has penetrated American education. Children appear to be more concerned with grades than learning. Even parents seem to be more concerned with their children's standing in the class than with their ability to become critical thinkers.

My brother-in-law has worked for a number of years as an elementary school teacher. In one of our conversations on education, he shared with me an incident that happened to him as a fourth-grade teacher.

A parent of one of his student's came in for a parent-teacher conference. The student was a bright student and had performed well in class. In fact, the child was a straight-A student. As the parent-teacher conference commenced, the parent inquired about his child's standing among the other students in the class. He wanted to know whether his child had the highest A average.

To his dismay, he discovered that there was one child with a higher grade. The parent lost control. He demanded an answer as to why his child wasn't the top student. My brother-in-law did the best he could to calm him. He assured him that the child was working well above his grade level, but that did not satisfy the parent. His child had to be number one. Can you imagine how much pressure that child must be under?

As a college professor, I see many students who enter college affected by this competitive pressure. The first question many ask upon entering my class is, What kind of grade can I get? Their major concern is whether or not the class will be a "GPA booster" (GPA=grade point average). This competitive atmosphere produces fact gatherers, trivia experts, information reservoirs, but not critical thinkers. It breeds unethical conduct. For many, a high GPA becomes more important than learning. How they get the grade and at what cost—that really doesn't matter.

This competitiveness in American education must stop. We must get back to our roots as a nation. The schools of our early history were staffed by teachers who believed that students came to or were sent to school to learn. Every effort was made to teach them. The one-room schools were impoverished, but they did provide an atmosphere for learning.

My mother was my fifth-grade teacher. That was the worst and best year of my life. I had learned how to make good grades by cheating. Oh, I was not a chronic cheater—just a crisis cheater. One day, I was not prepared for our daily spelling test, so I wrote the words in my hand. While taking the test, my mother noticed me looking down at my hand and called me to her desk.

It is an understatement to say that she was disappointed to find that I was cheating. But she didn't gloss it over. She didn't sweep it under the rug. My mother is from the old school, where learning is the most important thing. She saw potential in all students—not just the bright students. She knew that spelling was critical to learn. So she took out her leather strap and gave me a dozen or more licks on my hand in front of the whole class. This was my mother's method of punishment for any student caught cheating.

Later that day, my mother called me aside and said, "Son, you'll never learn by cheating, and it would be better for you to fail than to cheat." The words are etched in my brain forever. Many thanks go to my teacher—my mother—who was more concerned with learning than with grades. I got my one and only "D" that year, and naturally, it was in spelling. It was my worst academic year, but I could not have learned a better lesson. Education took on a new meaning. I was convinced about learning.

Competition Corrupts

Theo-Economics warns against the dangers of competition. It recommends instead motivating students to work up to their potential. Grades themselves are not bad, because they provide some means of evaluating learning progress. But Theo-Economics insists that grades not be the emphasis of education. Students should be rewarded for learning, not just for performing. Oral evaluation is a good way to test learning. Problem solving and group projects are other tools for evaluating students.

The concern in Theo-Economics is the training of human beings who are created in the image of God. Therefore, thinking students are the concern. Problem solving, creative thinking, and critical reasoning become the basis of true education. Read what one concerned educator has written:

> "Every human being created in the image of God is endowed with a power akin to that of the Creator—individuality, the power to think and to do. The men in whom this power is developed are the men who bear responsibilities, who are leaders in enterprise, and who influence character. It is the work of true education to develop this power, to train the youth to be thinkers, and not mere reflectors of other men's thought. Instead of confining their study to that which men have said or written, let students be directed to the sources of truth, to the vast fields opened for research in nature and revelation. Let them contemplate the great facts of duty and destiny, and the mind will expand and strengthen. Instead of educated weaklings, institutions of learning may send forth men strong to think and to act, men who are masters and not slaves of circumstances, men who possess breadth of mind, clearness of thought, and the courage of their convictions."[1]

More Academics, Less Athletics

Theo-Economics also recommends reevaluating the place of sports and extracurricular activities in education. There seems to be more emphasis these days on athletics than on academics. High school teachers confess to me the struggle many students have in balancing their extracurricular activities with their studies. Many evenings, students spend more time at football, baseball, basketball, and at cheerleader practice than they spend on doing their school work. Some schools are trying to foster a better learning environment with the "no pass, no play" rule, but the system still encourages more "play" than "pass." As a Theo-Economist, I see two problems.

First, sports encourages the spirit of competition, which we have already discovered is destroying our economy and our education. Students are encouraged, often times, to win at all costs. I am well aware of the many athletes who have made tremendous contributions to society. But I am gravely aware of what sports has done to the spirit of the American people. It is the same kind of spirit that brought Rome to its knees. This competitive spirit drives compassion from the heart. It teaches selfishness. It instills the concept of "rugged individualism" that keeps a nation from working together.

I know of a senior pastor who was an extremely good athlete in high school and college. But when he started working as a pastor, he quit playing sports. I noticed one day, as we were playing ping-pong, that he kept letting me win. I knew he was letting me win, because any time he decided to win a particular volley, he would win it. Now, don't get me wrong, I was no slouch at the ping-pong table. He was just very good.

After playing a while, I asked him, "Why are you letting me win."

"Why do I need to win?" he replied.

"'Cause that's what the game is about."

"Is it?"

With that, the pastor shared with me what sports had done to him. He was good at sports. But winning became everything. It drove any compassion for the loser from his heart. He saw himself becoming cold and indifferent to the feelings of others. And he decided to stop competing before he lost all compassion. Oh, he still plays a little sports here and there, but only for fun—not to compete.

Second, sports encourages an epicurean lifestyle. Pleasure becomes the goal of life. Hard work and learning take a back seat to pleasure and fun. Those of epicurean tastes invest more in pleasure than they do in education. Athletic programs in American education feed on this philosophy. Boys in our schools are real boys only if they are good in sports. Girls are not real girls unless they make the cheering squad. Parents will invest hundreds of dollars in high school athletic activities and then declare they have no money to send their children to college.

I am not suggesting that we cut out all sports in our schools. I myself am a great basketball fan. And even though I never became outstanding at sports, I do like to get out and play ball sometimes. I also understand the benefits of sports. Athletics provides exercise, which is much needed in the sedentary society we live in. Sports allow our youth to learn endurance, and, properly directed, can teach good work ethics.

But students must learn that the brain drives the body and that their greatest investment must be in educating their mind. They must understand that their success in life will be determined by how well they can apply knowledge and not by how well they play ball. The chance of becoming a professional athlete is perhaps one in a million.

I know that there are a lot of bright minds in our educational system, and as a Theo-Economist, I suggest we put more emphasis on academics and less on athletics—that we do more to foster the spirit of learning in our schools. We should teach our youth how to find as much enjoyment in learning as they do in sports. Which leads us to our next point. Who is teaching our children?

Higher Pay for Teachers

The backbone of any educational system is its teachers. Teachers can make or break a system. They can help students reach the pinnacle of knowledge—or they can send students to the depths of despair.

A few teachers have made a significant impact on my life. One of those was Dr. Mervin Warren, my homiletics teacher in college. He was the first to recognize my writing abilities. On one sermon manuscript, he wrote a note encouraging me to develop my writing ability. That one note was enough. Just the thought that my professor believed in me was enough to encourage me to believe in myself. His encouragement has resulted in the writing of many articles and now this book.

I think also of Dr. R. C. Sproul, one of my seminary professors. He made learning enjoyable and made me want to dig deeper and make larger contributions to the world. Then I remember Mrs. Siglar, my high school typing teacher. I didn't like typing and didn't see its value. But Mrs. Siglar was determined that I would learn to type. Without Mrs. Siglar's persistence, college and graduate school would have been far more difficult—and I certainly wouldn't be writing this book on a computer! But are we still attracting these kinds of people to the educational system?

Let me answer that question by turning back to where our nation invests its money. In most major cities in our country, the garbage man makes more money than the school teacher. We will pay a man $100,000.00 to entertain us by hitting a ball around an eighteen-hole golf course. Then we will argue about raising teachers' salaries. We will pay NFL and NBA players millions of dollars to play games. Then we vote down a fifty-cent property tax increase earmarked for education. Yet we have the nerve to demand the best teachers. How can we demand the best, when we are not willing to pay the price?

Writes R. C. Sproul:

> "The value of a teacher is placed at different levels in different societies. In America we tend to allow the value of the teacher to be dictated strictly by the marketplace factors. The teacher seems doomed by the iron law of wages, as the profession has experienced a glut with the surplus of teachers outnumbering positions available. The cliché is a byword, 'Teachers are a dime a dozen.' But it takes more than a certificate to be a good teacher. The former cliché may be answered by another, 'A good teacher is worth his weight in gold.' From a monetary value system,

the difference between a human being's weight in gold and a dime is astronomical. But we are a society who tends to measure the value of a professional by his salary level. From this perspective it is hard to attach much worth to the teacher."[2]

So what we have seen in the last couple of decades is a migration of our brighter minds to professions, trades, and businesses that pay higher salaries. Where once there was a teacher glut, now we don't have enough teachers. I have heard some colleges considering closing down the education department because they don't have enough education majors to justify having a department.

One day I stopped a fifteen-year-old male member in my church and asked him what he planned to do with his life. I had watched him for quite a while and felt that God was calling him into the ministry.

"Pastor", he said, "I'm planning to be a lawyer."

"Is that what you really want to be?" I queried.

"Yes, sir," he muttered, with hesitancy in his voice.

"Young man, I believe God has called you to the ministry! Have you considered going to Oakwood College and studying for the ministry?" I asked with conviction.

"Yes, sir, but I've decided against it, because I can't make enough money in the ministry to support my aging mother," he earnestly replied.

I've heard the same sentiments expressed over and over again by students who might have considered a career in education. What a sad commentary on the value system of today's society!

Teachers were once among the most revered professionals in the country, but they now have little prestige or respect. In America, that is. Sproul, who did graduate work in Europe, says that many nations still place teachers on the upper rungs of the professional ladder. He also explains that historically, the teaching profession was held in high esteem. Taking a note about teachers from the Bible, Sproul writes:

> "The Bible is not silent about the role of the teacher. It is by divine mandate that we are called to give honor to our teachers. The role of the teacher in Israel was one of elevated status. Jewish jokes abound about the pride of the Yiddish mother who

speaks of 'my son, the doctor,' or 'my son, the attorney.' In Israel, the materfamilias spoke with the greatest pride when she could say, 'my son, the rabbi.' So highly elevated was the status of the teacher that it had the power to reverse traditional matters of family etiquette. In the Jewish home the father was treated with solemn outward signs of respect. His authority was acknowledged by visible signs of acquiescence. It was the custom for every child to stand when the father entered the room. That custom was broken on only one occasion. If the son was a rabbi, then it was the father who was required to stand when the son entered the room."[3]

I personally believe, as a Theo-Economist, that teachers ought to be among the highest-paid professionals in this country. I believe we need to bring dignity back to the teaching profession by increasing salaries. That way, we can start once again attracting the cream of the crop.

By the way, if you are concerned about people being motivated by money, studies have shown that in the long run, people stay in a profession not because of the money but because they find fulfillment in their job. There are hundreds of stories of people who have given up lucrative jobs to do more fulfilling and rewarding work, even though the pay was less. There are money-grubbers in every profession. But what higher salaries will do is to give teachers tangible evidence that we value them enough to allow them the opportunity to do what they love to do without financial frustration.

Education for Head, Heart, and Hand

Theo-Economics stands in the Hebraic tradition. In the Jewish economy, the educational system was broad based. Education was to involve the student's head, heart, and hand. No Jewish family would allow its children to grow up without a well-rounded education. In fact, even if a student was extremely gifted in academics, he was still required to learn a trade.

You see, in the Jewish economy, there was no such thing as an unproductive child. To allow a child to grow up without learning a trade was considered a sin. Parents believed that sending a child out into the world without a trade was like sending him out to be a criminal. Some kind of skill with the hands was thought of as a safeguard against unemployment. A child could always make a living with his hands.

But today's educational system mainly concentrates on the hand, to the detriment of both the economy and the child. Theo-Economics is convinced that we need three types of education for all students.

1. A liberal-arts education — Education for the head.
2. Trades — Education for the hands.
3. Common sense — Education for the heart.

Dr. E. B. Dubois and Professor Booker T. Washington, two leading African-American educators, were constantly at odds as to what kind of education would best suit the African-American community. Booker T. Washington argued that Black people needed to learn trades. He saw trades — carpentry, brick masonry, plumbing, agriculture — as providing an economic base or an economy for Black people.

But Dubois argued that our Black young people needed to fill their heads with noble ideas and power information. The Black race needed leaders, and for Dubois, leadership came through the training of the head and not the hand. Dubois was not totally against trades, and neither was Washington totally against book learning. It was simply a matter of where each placed his emphasis.

But as I observe the needs of today's young people, I believe the educational views of both Dubois and Washington are needed. I believe the Hebraic concept is a must. Our schools, as already mentioned, need to push for high levels of academic learning. This should by done not by putting pressure on teachers to raise test scores, which are not accurate measures for what a child knows, but by inspiring and requiring students to read more. I believe that reading is the best way for teachers to challenge students with learning for the head. I think it is interesting that the master teacher, Jesus, left a book for us to read so we might learn His lessons.

In the earlier days of our nation, most of our institutions of higher education were industrial training schools. Academics were required but so was the learning of some type of trade. The education of the hand was an important part of the educational process. I still believe that trades are important. Not everyone is called to be a teacher, doctor, preacher, or lawyer. Some are called to a trade. The educational system should provide for that type of student. But even those called to professions should know how to use their hands to support themselves.

Of course, trades today must reflect the high-tech age we live in. The traditional trades of carpentry, brick masonry, electrical work, plumbing, and welding are still important, but we must add trades that are a part of this computer age.

Then finally, we must focus on the education of the heart. This is what people in bygone days called "mother wit" or "common sense." But you and I both know that common sense is no longer common. Many people, young and old, have much head knowledge but don't know how to apply it. In Theo-Economics, we call this practical application of knowledge "common sense." In higher education we call it "critical thinking."

But whatever it is called, there is a great dearth of it in today's world. This kind of education is more caught than taught. It comes from the study of human nature—not from a psychology textbook, but from personal observance of life. It comes from sitting back and listening to others. It comes from spending time with older people. It comes from thinking. And all three of these things are rarely encouraged in modern education.

When I was growing up, we were told that "children are to be seen and never to be heard." This was a poetic way of telling children to shut up and listen. But nowadays, children are encouraged to express themselves, to speak out, to have an opinion.

I believe the Lord knew what He was doing when He gave us two ears and one mouth. Young people must be encouraged, like adults, to do more listening. The best place to start the education of the heart is by spending time with senior citizens. Locked away in the hearts of many senior citizens is the wisdom of years.

Unlike past generations, we don't put much value on the

elderly. But from personal experience, I know that older people have a really important role to play in educating the hearts of our youth. Students should be required to spend time with a sage in their community as a part of their classwork.

Finally, students should be required to think and write about the deeper issues of life. This experience gives students the opportunity to crystalize their thoughts, thus helping to produce wisdom—"common sense."

Education is a cheap investment by comparison with the high cost of ignorance. It is lack of education that keeps unemployment high. When people are not trained, their talents and abilities cannot be turned into productive energy. People who are unemployed are more inclined to satisfy their unmet needs through crime and violence.

Money spent to deal with crime and violence in America dwarfs the little we spend in education. We spend more on incarcerating criminals than we do on educating children. It costs about $30,000 to keep one man behind bars for a year. The most we spend per child in education is around $6,000 annually. From a purely dollars-and-cents point of view, it is far cheaper to educate a man than to incarcerate him.

I hope that in this chapter I've caused you to do some serious thinking about education in this country. Education is important to the prosperity, preservation, and protection of our nation. Let's makes some bigger investments in it.

Checkpoint

■ Let's stop the "brain drain" going on in American education.

■ Many students are getting grades but not an education.

■ Theo-Economics reminds us of the value of education — the foundation of any sound economy.

■ Competition is another aspect of evolution and is corrupting our educational system.

■ Our students need more academics and less athletics.

■ Increasing the pay of teachers will show our renewed commitment to education and our elevated view of the teacher.

■ There must be education of the heart, head, and hand.

■ Education is cheaper than incarceration.

8

The American Dream— or the American Nightmare?

The Great American Dream is owning your own home. It is having property you can call your own. But is the American Dream a realistic dream? Is owning your own home all it is cracked up to be?

I believe there are myths about owning your own home and property that have turned the American Dream into the American Nightmare. Here are some of the myths I believe have turned dreams into nightmares:

1. You can't build wealth without owning property.
2. It's cheaper to buy than to rent.
3. Property is the best investment.
4. Investing in property is a hedge against inflation.
5. There is no more property being made.

These myths appear to have the ring of truth, but on closer inspection, we discover that they are clouds without rain. Let's examine each myth individually.

You Cannot Build Wealth Without Property

Few understand the secrets of building wealth in America. We are told to work hard, buy some land, and wealth will come. I won't spend time in this book explaining how to build wealth in America. But in my upcoming book *Turn Your Talent Into Cash,* I will detail how to make money and remain moral. Right now, understand that "wealth is in the mind, not in property." Property doesn't make money. Ideas for the use of property are where money is made in America. I know people who own many acres of land but don't have a dime. I know others who have wealth but own little, if any, property.

Now let me make it clear—people do make money in real estate. The records document that fact. But it wasn't the property per se that made the money. It was the person's ability to see potential. It was an idea for the use of the land that created the wealth. Think about it! Does property produce money on its own?

People make money in real estate by selling it, farming it, developing it, or speculating in it. Every one of these methods of making money in property calls for ideas and energy. And people who do well in real estate have a natural talent for dealing in property. They have a keen eye for property potential. They are usually excellent negotiators. They are risk takers and can handle failure and loss relatively easily. Dealing in property isn't for everyone.

So don't be fooled! The gurus of the "wealth through real estate" concept are making their big money from seminars, tapes, books, and videos—ideas. Sure, there are people making money in property. But for every one who makes money in real estate, there are hundreds of others who have lost their shirts.

The belief of many is that there are only a few ways to build wealth and that property is one of them. The truth is that there are literally thousands of honest, legitimate, God-inspired ways to make money. There are as many ways to make money as there are different talents and gifts. I have talked with real estate brokers and have read about those who own lots of property. And I have discovered that for most, it was not the property that made them money. It was the ideas centered on their gifts and talents and put into the marketplace, that created wealth for them. Property was just a by-product of making money. Real estate, for these people, is simply a repository for their wealth.

A good illustration of what I'm talking about is seen in the fast-food industry. If property is so profitable, why don't McDonalds, Burger King, Taco Bell, and Subway go out and buy up large tracts of land on which to open up their restaurants? If you will take notice, these companies only lease or buy enough acreage to do business — no more. They understand that their profits are in the products — not in the property. Less property = less responsibility = less taxes. "It's the bread that makes the bread."

Theo-Economics takes the mystery out of wealth building. The secret is investing in and developing one's God-given talents. It is recognizing that God gives the power and the ability to produce wealth. Remember, "Wealth is in the mind, not in the property." People who understand this can lose all their property and wealth and, with a creative mind, win it all back again. Wealth, indeed, is created in the mind.

Modern economists seem timid about telling people this secret. They appear afraid to release citizens to reach their potential of creating wealth. They seem not to want to inform the general public that "Wealth is in the mind." Many in our nation's history understood this secret. Henry Ford became wealthy with the idea of mass producing an economical car. Thomas Edison became wealthy with his many inventions. Booker T. Washington became famous and prosperous from his ideas about peanuts — not property. Property is not wealth. It simply has the potential of producing wealth.

So before you buy into the American Dream, check to see if you have a real idea and plan to make property work for you. Don't be a fool — know the rule: "Wealth is in the mind — not in the property."

It's Cheaper to Buy Than to Rent

This myth has been the downfall of many families—especially young couples. It has caused many to jump blindly and prematurely into home ownership. Home ownership can be a boom or a bust. It can be a dream come true or a hairy nightmare that you never awaken from. George Fooshee, Jr., in his book, *You Can Be Financially Free*, states:

> "Americans have been rushing into the unknown in home buying ever since the end of World War II. Owning your own home has been the dream of most young couples. The big justification question is: 'Why pay all that rent and end up with nothing?' Following this question comes the positive justification: 'You might as well be buying your home as pouring all that rent down the drain.'"[1]

This myth carries with it enormous social pressure. People are made to feel foolish for renting. "You mean to tell me you are still renting?" is the famous make-me-feel-like-a-failure punch. Many are in the 'Keep up with the Joneses' syndrome already, and the make-me-feel-like-a-failure punch knocks them out.

Alfred W. Munzert, in his book *Poor Richard's Economic Survival Manual*, writes:

> "Today, inflation, scarcity of money and prohibitively high interest rates have all but excluded the vast majority of Americans—particularly young couples seeking their first home—from achieving home ownership. In desperation, many young couples are entering into agreements that can only end in disaster.
>
> "For example, a former student of mine wrote to me not long ago from a city in the midwest. After four years of penny-pinching struggle, she and her husband had managed to save $10,000, which they used as a down payment on a $72,000 home, a modest 3-bedroom ranch home. Elated at being homeowners, they happily glossed over the enormous and potentially destructive obligation they had undertaken."

Munzert goes on to describe the young couple's unrecognized dilemma:

"Given the term and interest rate of their mortgage, I calculated that they would ultimately pay more than $250,000 for their home! Moreover, with a combined annual income of $25,000, the monthly payment of $734.00 per month (plus taxes) will take 40 percent of their total income. Should either of them become ill or lose their job—they will possibly forfeit the house and all their investment.

"In a similar situation, still another couple in a nearby town—and with even less income—have committed themselves to monthly payments of over $800.00 per month, roughly 50 percent of their income!

"Such purchases are almost certain prescriptions for disaster."[2]

My heart aches when I think of the many young couples I know that are in similar or maybe even worse situations and who still believe the myth that "buying is cheaper than renting."

Is buying cheaper than renting? Yes and no. It depends on what kind of house you buy, how much you put down on the house, how much you have in savings that you can devote to maintenance, and how long you plan to stay in the house.

What many fail to take into consideration is that the cost of home ownership is more than just paying the monthly mortgage. Maintenance, repairs, lawn care, pest control, and utilities (they are usually more when owning than when renting) all must be factored into the cost of home ownership.

When renting, on the other hand, you know what your housing costs are—at least during the period of the rental agreement. A number of books on the market can help determine which is cheaper for you. My point is that buying isn't always cheaper and that renters are not all losers. Investigate before you jump into home ownership.

Property Is a Hedge Against Inflation

All of us are concerned about inflation. Inflation robs the value of our money right from under our noses. But is owning property a hedge against inflation? Many hard-working citizens appear to believe this myth. But they know little, if anything, about inflation. Clearing up this myth begins by understanding inflation. Allow Alfred Munzert to explain this oft-misunderstood topic:

"Inflation is at once the most destructive and cruelest of all economic situations. It is also the least understood by the average person. The real cause — and the only cause of inflation is an increase in the money supply (in our case, the paper money supply) — without a corresponding increase in the production of goods and services. Since the government controls the money supply, the government controls inflation and it could stop it overnight.

"To demonstrate just how an increase in the money supply creates inflation, we shall use a simple illustration:

"Let us suppose that you live in a small town of, say 500 people. The town is quite self-sufficient, and everyone is gainfully employed in one of the small local business or industries. No one is wealthy, but the cost of living is reasonable and everyone is quite comfortable. It is a very desireable place to live.

"On the south side of town are twenty very desirable building lots. You plan to buy one in the future and build a new home upon it. These are the last remaining lots in the village, but there is no cause for hurry. The population is quite stable and is not expected to grow. These beautiful one-acre lots sell for $500.00 each and this price also been stable for many years.

"Suddenly, however, a large and wealthy group of visitors arrives. They like the town and decide to stay. The price of the 20 lots begins to rise dramatically — from $500 to $1000, to $2000 and up as these new arrivals begin to bid against each other.

"This rise in the price of the lots — inflation — is due to the fact that you have had a sudden increase in the supply of money in town without an increase in the number of lots to be purchased.

"Inflation, then, is simply an increase in the money supply without increased production. More dollars chasing fewer goods automatically causes prices to rise. . . . In short, there is an excess of dollars floating through the society and bidding up the cost of every item. It is the government's calculated printing and distribution of millions of excess paper dollars that is the sole cause of our growing inflation and the destruction of each individual's purchasing power."[3]

In the last couple of decades, there has been a steady decline in the value of the dollar and a growing rate of inflation. Right now, the inflation rate hovers between 4 percent and 6 percent. The return on a home investment is about 3 percent (if your property is well maintained and it's in the right location). It doesn't take a genius to see that homeowners are not keeping up with inflation. And the more our nation shoots up in debt, the higher inflation will rise and the more homeowners will lag behind on the return on their investment. But that's only part of the equation.

We all have discovered the fact that it takes more dollars to buy less in today's economy. Understanding this simple fact should help us to see that home ownership isn't what it used to be. Buying a home with inflated money makes it difficult, maybe even impossible, for property to be a hedge against inflation.

Runaway inflation in the seventies and the early eighties made home ownership attractive as a hedge against inflation. Many couples took the big plunge and bought homes. But unlike home buyers of previous generations who bought with the idea of staying in one location at least until the children left home, home buyers during the seventies and eighties bought with an eye toward investment.

Their plan was this: Buy a starter a home. Live in it for a few years. Sell it for a sizeable profit. Reinvest the profit in a bigger home. Live in that one for a few years. Sell this home for an even larger profit. Keep reinvesting until you could purchase the "dream home."

During my college years, I lived in Alabama. I can remember in the early seventies that three-bedroom houses were selling for under $17,000. After college, I moved away from Alabama, but returned to the mid-South to work at the end of the seventies. The houses that had been selling for under $17,000 before I left the area were now being purchased for over $30,000. I stayed in the mid-South until the early nineties. By then, those same houses were selling for just under $70,000.

But what many failed to see was that even though they received sizeable equity returns on their homes, it was costing more to get into another house. Add to the inflated prices the high interest rates on mortgages, and what you had was an illusion of increased value. In the west and east during the same period, increases were even more phenomenal. But it was not only inflation that drove up prices, but speculation by greedy Americans seeking to "get rich quick," helping to send the cost of housing through the ceiling.

As the "Roaring Eighties" came to a close, the chickens started coming home to roost. Inflated home prices began to drop. And all around the country, homeowners saw their property values take drastic plunges. All the while, the myth of home ownership as a hedge against inflation lived on. I am amazed at the way so many people don't want to wake up out of their nightmares. No matter how you look at it, home ownership is not always a hedge against inflation.

Now, don't get upset. I know that home ownership is the American Dream. I realize that ownership of property is our national "sacred cow," and I am by no means seeking to discourage people from buying homes. My purpose is simply to help us all think clearly about home ownership. Believe it or not, I do see positive benefits in home ownership. I'm just concerned that we capture the ghost that keeps turning the American Dream into the American Nightmare.

I look at home ownership as I do car ownership. I know that buying a car is a poor investment. Every time I drive my car, it depreciates. But for my lifestyle and work, owning a car is a necessity. Do I not buy a car, then, because it is not the best investment? Of course not. I go out and buy the car. But my knowledge about the various kinds of investments dictates what kind of car I buy. I buy a pre-owned car, allowing someone else to take part of the depreciation. I pay cash, if possible, for the car—or finance as low an amount as possible over no more than thirty-six months. This way, I keep a poor investment from become a horrible investment.

In buying a house, don't be fooled. A house is a necessity. But take the time to understand why you are buying the house. You buy a house to live in, not to speculate with.

What we must come to understand is that property was never intended by God to be a hedge against inflation. God never intended for property to be a means of getting rich. Property, in Theo-Economics, is simply a place where God allows us to develop. The purpose of home ownership is to teach responsibility. As we manage our own homesteads, it helps us develop character. House cleaning, the care of the lawn, house repairs, and the general maintenance of property call for the use of virtues such as diligence, integrity, faithfulness, thrift, patience, and hard work—necessities for success in every area of life. A family that keeps a disorderly home is normally disorderly in other areas of life. And this same disorderliness keeps them from being financially independent. The Bible says it this way: "Well done, good and faithful servant! You have been faithful with a few things; I will put you in charge of many things. Come and share your master's happiness!" (Matthew 25:21.)

This is what owning property is all about—developing as stewards.

The best inflation fighter is not property, but potential. Personal potential, developed and used to create wealth. Remember that "Wealth is in the mind, not in property."

Property Is the Best Investment

I have heard this all my life and believed it, just like many other uninformed Americans. And like millions of others, I too took the plunge and bought my first house. Everyone reassured me that buying a home was the best investment a couple could make. But is property the best investment?

Few take the time to talk to the hundreds of thousands of people who have lost everything through investing in property. Even the banking community began to believe the myth. In the late seventies and eighties, inflated real estate prices convinced even the bankers that you can't go wrong in real estate. In earlier days, commercial banks and savings-and-loan companies were very conservative about lending money on property. But during the boom, these lending institutions themselves speculated in property—large home mortgages, apartment complexes, office buildings, skyscrapers.

Now look at the mess! Every one of us on the tax rolls of America is paying the bill for what is now known as "the S & L bailout." Why? Because men believed that property was the best investment. Of course, we know that greed, corruption, and the lust for power had its part to play in the failures of the S & L's, but none of it could have happened without the belief that you can't lose in real estate.

I found out the hard way, like many other Americans, that property is the not the best investment. After saving for a number of years, we bought our first house. It was a nice little home. Three bedrooms, two baths, and about thirteen hundred square feet in a nice neighborhood. We invested about $5,000 to get into the house—a $2,500 down payment and $2,500 in closing fees. The house cost $50,000. We financed $47,500 on a thirty-year mortgage.

For seven years we lived in that house, paying on the mortgage. Then I accepted a job in another state. We put the house on the market to sell, and after a year and four failed contracts, we finally sold the house for what we owed on it—$45,000! Can you believe it? After seven years and about $36,000 in payments, I had only reduced my original mortgage by $2,500. Including the repairs and maintenance on the house, my wife and I had invested around $50,000.

Who won on that deal? It surely wasn't me. But I believed, like the majority of Americans, that property was the best investment. Please don't misunderstand me! I am not discouraging the purchase of a home. I know we need a place to stay. My point is this: Don't buy a house or property based on myths that cloud the truth about that property. Clearly think through your reasons for buying. Plan carefully how you will go about purchasing real estate. Save as much as you can for the down payment. Taking out as small a mortgage as possible for a short period of time helps to prevent the American Dream from becoming the American Nightmare.

Let me close this section with a quote of Peter Wolf from his book, *Land in America, Its Value, Use and Control*:

> "I am troubled, then, by the prevalent assumption, made with considerable assurance by so many people, that the past per-

formance of land as an investment will protect their assets from inflation and provide for future profit. And I am troubled by a continuing belief in other concurrent underlying assumptions that have for so long fueled a passion for land as an investment. The assumptions remain, while new and decisive conditions in America are ignored."[4]

They Aren't Making Any More Land

This final myth probably is the clincher of all the property myths. "They aren't making any more land." What a convincing argument about the value of land! It gives the distinct impression that we are running out of land — that land, like other natural resources, is becoming scarce. This myth has caused people to rush into purchases without thinking. It has caused men and women to hoard land, to risk their lives for land, and to place all their security in land. This myth has brought on wars and strife.

Wolf quotes Margaret Mitchell, in her classic, *Gone With the Wind*, where she had the Southern plantation owner Gerald O'Hara impress upon his daughter:

"Land is the only thing in the world that amounts to anything . . . for 'tis the only thing in this world that lasts, and don't you be forgetting it! 'Tis the only thing worth working for, worth fighting for — worth dying for. . ."[5]

Modern economists perpetuate this myth by writing it in textbooks and teaching it as truth. Will Rogers made this myth popular when he advised the whole country: "Buy land. They ain't making any more of the stuff."

What is astonishing is that unbeknown to American citizens, this myth strikes at the very idea of the existence of a personal God. The idea that no more land is being made suggests that God is no longer creating. It implies that God has stopped His creative activity in the world. It conveys the idea of a deistic God.

In his book, *The Reign of God*, Richard Rice writes:

"Deism attributes the origin of the world to God, but it denies that He has any present interest in its activity. Like a master craftsman, God started the universe running. Since He designed it perfectly, He never needs to adjust its operation. The common metaphor for this view of God is the absentee landlord. It suggests that God is ultimately or originally responsible for the existence of the world, but He takes no part in its current operation. In a deistic world view, there is no place for supernatural revelation and miraculous intervention. Everything operates according to fixed natural laws."[6]

The Theo-Economist believes that God, the "Invisible Hand," is clearly involved in the world—that God is immanent, meaning that He is personally involved in the world. Yes, God is transcendent, standing out above the world as the mighty God, but He is loving enough to take an active role in the affairs of men.

We can still expect to see God's creative power as an active force in the world. He rested after six days of creation but never stopped creating. Every time the trees shed their winter coats and slip into their summer wear, God is creating. Every time the sun creeps back up over the eastern horizon, God is creating. Every time a mother gives birth to a newborn child, God is creating. If in fact God is active in other parts of nature, we can be sure He is creatively active in real estate.

When I speak of God's continued creation in the world, I am referring both to God's creation of something from nothing and His use of already created material to make something. Both are supernatural actions of God.

It is just as much a miracle of God when a zygote and a sperm combine to make a child as when God stooped down to pick up clay and made a man. It takes the same creative power to bring grass from seeds planted in the ground as it did to speak grass into existence in the beginning.

In real estate, we can see God's creative power still at work. The state of Florida contains almost thirty-seven million acres of land—much of it swamps and lakes. Millions of acres of Florida's swamp land, once uninhabitable, have been drained and filled to create new available acres for use.

Another source of new land is islands. Two-thirds of the earth is covered with water. At the bottom of all oceans is earth, land, terra firma. From time to time, God's allows volcanic activity to take place on the ocean floor, which results in the emergence of visible islands. *National Geographic* magazine carried an article that shows how these new islands appear from the ocean floor.

This creation of land is as much a result of God's creative power as is the birth of a child or the growth of trees. And since God is God, He is not limited to using existing material. If there ever came a time when God needed to start from scratch in creating new land for us, He could do that too. It is imperative that we understand this, because it helps eliminate some of the urgency about owning property. You don't have to go out to buy today. There will always be property available at an affordable price when it's time for you to buy. There is no scarcity of land in America. Peter Wolf writes:

"Except as the very best locations in the few fast-growing spots, there is no shortage of land in America. The raw land stretches out across a massive continent of 2.3 billion acres. Of this, 900 million acres are owned by one level of government or another. The federal government, as the largest landlord in the nation, owns about one third of the country's land. This land alone, if ever needed, could be released in the the marketplace as a surplus commodity. Cropland covers about 400 million acres, of which a great deal is idle. Empty grasslands, idle pastures, and vast ranges claim some 600 million acres. Forest land, much of it poorly managed and relatively unproductive, consumes 400 million acres. Over 100 million acres are wilderness, federal and state parks, reservations, wildlife refuges, and defense and flood-control areas; this land is also empty and, except in rare instances, under utilized . . . In the metropolitan areas of America today there exist huge, available land reserves. According to the 1970 United States census, only 10 percent of the land contained within the metropolitan areas of the United States was fully developed. Since then new development has continued at a significant pace, but surely not rapidly enough to raise this figure by more than one or at the most two percent. Estimates vary, but without any question, as much as one half of all the so-called developed land inside metropolitan areas is under-utilized."[7]

Theo-Economics understands that this myth of the scarcity

of property is what brings the fear of not having — or the greed for owning — property in America. This fear keeps people competing and fighting over land. It fuels foolish speculation in property. It contributes to the over-extension of personal finances of many American citizens in order to own property.

Ultimately, what people are looking for is security. They are hoping to find it in owning property. But Theo-Economics teaches that there is no security in property — either as an investment for the future, as a hedge against inflation, or even as a permanent place to live. Owning property is just God's way of teaching us responsibility. But it is never to be our security!

What kind of security is property in an earthquake? How secure does one feel when he is behind on property taxes? When the mortgage falls behind on the house, how much security does one have then? I believe our founding fathers understood this. That is why they had engraved on our money the words, "In God We Trust," not "In Property We Trust."

In Theo-Economics, purchasing property can be a positive step, provided myths are quashed and caution is not thrown to the winds. Owning property can become that "American Dream" if you understand the real purpose of property. Again, the primary purpose of owning property is to help us learn responsibility. I know this sounds strange. What does responsibility have to do with owning property?

Property is a talent. And like any other God-given talent, it must be developed. How one uses a talent determines its value. Therefore, each individual is personally held accountable for the success or failure of the talent of property. In other words, when you purchase property, you accept responsibility for its improvement or lack of improvement. Property, like any other talent, is valuable only as it is improved. That is why I can say that the primary purpose of property is to teach us responsibility.

Some may have a talent for writing, but if they never publish anything, it is of no value to them or to anyone else. A person may have the world's greatest singing voice, but if he or she doesn't improve it and take it out to the marketplace, its value will diminish.

I see people all the time jumping into property who have been misled by these prevalent myths mentioned in this chapter — many of them knowing next to nothing about the responsibility that comes with owning property. Therefore, many are neither financially or mentally prepared to take on this large responsibility. The "American Dream" becomes then the "American Nightmare."

Scores — thousands — of people across this country have lost all because they didn't know the purpose of property. They didn't understand that "Wealth is in the mind, not in the property." Therefore, instead of buying land with ideas about how to make it profitable, they bought it thinking that it had value just because it was land. They bought houses with the belief that a house is valuable just because it is a house, not understanding that a house is only worth something if it is maintained. They bought without understanding that the value of property, to a great extent, is in direct proportion to how much responsibility one takes for its care, maintenance, and improvement. So many have been rudely awakened when their dream turned into a nightmare.

But I have seen others who understood the purpose of property. They didn't see it as security or a hedge against inflation or a way to build wealth. So all their dreams were not tied to property. They built their wealth through developing ideas centered on their talents and gifts. And they found security in God — not in the property. So if their property failed (and we have seen many lose everything in natural disasters), they wouldn't fail.

The bottom line is this: Property can be a boom or a bust. It can be blessing or a curse. It all depends on how responsible you are.

9

The National Addiction

Addictions of any kind are horrible. They leave their victims powerless and enslaved. The scourge of alcohol and drug addiction in this country makes headline news and causes great concern. But debt is the greatest addiction our nation faces, yet few take this addiction seriously.

The national debt in this country is nearing four trillion dollars and growing rapidly. Our nation and many of its people appear so addicted to credit that some are apparently convinced that our nation cannot prosper without debt. Modern economists perpetuate the idea by writing from their ivory towers that a certain amount of debt is good for the country—that deficit spending allows the economy to keep expanding at respectable levels, thus keeping employment and production high.

But the injection of inflated money (borrowed money, debt) into the economy as a means of stimulation, as modern economists suggest, is like a drug addict injecting a shot of heroin into his veins. It gives the immediate desired result—a high—but it has long-term negative consequences.

Just as drug addiction destroys its victims, debt addiction too, eventually brings a nation and its people to their knees. It sucks the very lifeblood out of the economy. It saps the wealth of the nation. This is because the lifeblood of any economy is people—human beings. Debt has a negative impact on people. It is just as deadly as any drug.

I have been in helping professions all my working career and have had an opportunity to observe what debt is doing to people. I have watched homes wrecked by debt. Statistics fail to tell the whole story. They can only tell us that 97 percent of all marriages that end in divorce list financial problems and debt as the major cause of the breakup. The statistics don't communicate the anger, rage, hurt, loneliness, depression, and loss of dignity these victims feel. They don't disclose how job efficiency and productivity are affected by what has happened to credit-aholics. They don't show how these debt victims pull on the frayed hems of the nation's economic garments by adding to the welfare rolls.

I watch as the huge American consumer debt of over $794 billion takes its toll on the health of workers. The leading cause of death in America is heart disease. The leading cause of heart disease is stress—and the negative lifestyle choices stressed people tend to make. And the leading cause of stress in America is financial problems—mainly debt.

Finally, I have observed that many people in debt apparently become brain dead. Debt is not just an addiction—it is also a type of slavery. And slavery of any kind affects the mind. I have watched individuals in debt lose almost all their creative thinking abilities. They walk around like zombies from one financial crisis to another, too depressed to create wealth for themselves or the nation.

So the debt crisis in this country is not just about our national debt, but about the way of life we Americans have grown accustomed to living. This way of life is a continuing flirtation with a mortgaged future. It is a failure to accept the fact that into each life (country) a little rain must fall. We fail to learn that suffering, hard times, self-denial, and even pain are a natural part of human existence. So with the help of contemporary economists, we enter into debt to avoid suffering or to keep from denying ourselves things we think we deserve. Like the Mediprin commercial, "We haven't got time for the pain."

Theo-Economics teaches us how to live with suffering and sacrifice, with increases and decreases, with boom and bust. Theo-Economics doesn't paint a picture of an ever-expanding economy. It teaches us that because of sin, the earth experiences cycles. Spring follows winter. "As long as the earth endures, seed time and harvest, cold and heat, summer and winter, day and night will never cease" (Genesis 8:22).

The great scientists and engineers of our nation have studied the graceful flight of the bird in nature and have built airplanes that soar above the clouds. They have investigated the sub-aquatic skills of the fish and created submarines that go thousands of feet under the sea for months at a time. But somehow, they have allowed God's economic principles in nature to elude them.

It seems we have closed our eyes to the lessons to be learned about economics from the cycles of nature. As much as we like summer and spring, winter does come. So in human economy, as much as we enjoy boom times, recessions and depressions do come. There are winters (downturns) in every economy.

Unproductive Responses to Recession

There are two unproductive responses to economic cycles;

1. Denial of the cycle.
2. Attempting to alter or stop the cycle.

The first response of denial is that of most American citizens. We just don't believe that economic winters will come. We think the summer of prosperity will always be here. So we never plan for economic downturns. We spend all our reserves and run up all our charge accounts as if summer will last forever.

The average American appears to live as if in a fantasy world — where no one ever loses a job, no one ever gets sick, everyone looks out for your best interests, the sun always shines, and even the rain is liquid goodness. And when winter hits, as it always does, our only solution to the chilling winds of economic downturns is to borrow and go deeper in debt. Debt addiction and debt disaster are the consequences of denying the cycles of nature. It is a sad commentary on the many who live with their heads in the sand.

The second unproductive response is to attempt to alter or stop the cycle of nature. This group is made up of modern economists and contemporary politicians. They understand that economic winters will come. They read and study diligently all of the latest data on the economic weather front. And they have a pretty good idea of what the future weather is going to be. But instead of planning for downturns in the economy, instead of preparing people and provisions for the winter of an economic downturn, they spend their time writing up econometric formulas, trying in vain to prevent economic winters from coming.

This is what deficit spending is all about. It is the government's attempt to hold back the economic winter. Flooding the economy with inflated dollars and devising make-work programs are vain attempts of economists and politicians to hold back old man winter. But try as they may, when the snow of inflation begins to fall and the chilly winds of economic downturn and depression start to blow, the experts cannot stop them.

How would a weatherman look writing up formulas and proposals to prevent a hurricane from striking? The weatherman can predict—but cannot prevent. He can tell us how to prepare for the hurricane, but we surely don't expect him to forestall it. Modern economists attempt to forecast our economic future (though the truth is that they are even worse at predicting than the weatherman), but they can never stop economic bad times.

Theo-Economics teaches us that we must accept economic winters just as we do the winters in nature. It teaches us that success comes not in stopping the winter but in being prepared for it. We learn that economic winters are just as inevitable as economic summers. So the best way to be ready for winter is not just knowing when it will come but taking preventive measures in order to ride it out.

Not until I was ten years of age did I experience my first real winter. We moved to Michigan from the south, and for the first time in my life, I saw real snow. That first winter, my brothers, sister, and I—along with our parents—rolled in the snow, ate the snow, made figures in the snow, and had snowball fights. It was all great fun—that is, until we had to shovel the snow from the driveways. Then snow became work.

As the winter dragged on and we had to push the car out of snowdrifts, bundle up tightly before going outside, and shovel more driveways, I longed for the summer time. And when it came, I never wanted it to leave. But wishing, hoping, and even praying couldn't keep the winter from coming. Nature will run its cyclic course.

I noticed though, that the city fathers didn't join me in simply wishing for the winter not to come. Instead, all summer long, they checked their inventories for winter preparation. To make it through the winter, the city's leaders knew that snowplows had to be in working condition, that salt spreaders had to be in perfect repair, and that huge stockpiles of salt and sand had to be gathered to combat old man winter.

It was evident they couldn't stop the winter from coming, but they certainly could make it through the winter by being prepared. And prepared they were. At the first sign of winter, the city salt crews were put on alert. And when the first snowflake fell, the salt trucks would hit the street, not stopping until every major thoroughfare was salted. Winters don't bother midwesterners, because they prepare for it.

The Reasons for the National Addiction

Why is our nation suffering from the tremors of debt addiction? Why aren't we handling economic winters? There are at least three reasons for America's oversize debt.

1. Lack of national vision.
2. The "get-rich-quick" philosophy.
3. Waste.

First, we lack a national vision. Theo-Economics knows the importance of vision—of setting and reaching for goals. "Where there is no vision, the people perish" (Proverbs 29:18, KJV). Goal-directed vision is what fuels any economy. Vision provides direction. It informs action. It makes work purposeful. It gives rationale to self-sacrifice and self-control.

Politicians talk about the vision of a stronger America, but where is it? No wonder Americans have not been willing to sacrifice and control their spending. Politicians and economists have focused on the problems of the nation, but beyond the lip service they give it, where is their vision for the nation? Where are the positive goals for the nation? Where is the vision of hope for our great country? To get America to turn from its debt addiction, leaders must set aside partisan politics and carve out a vision. We must fix what is wrong with our nation, but a simple, pragmatic approach to leading it will not move people to make the kind of sacrifices needed to strengthen our ailing economy. To get this nation back on a sound economic footing, a clear and positive vision must be outlined.

As a financial counselor, I have helped many couples overcome financial reverses. My greatest struggle has been in helping them set positive goals. Many of them could not see beyond their financial dilemma. The problems kept them from finding the answers. Positive goals (vision) help us see that it is worth making the sacrifice and controlling spending. I believe that if the people of this country could see how sacrificing would pay off, they would be willing to sacrifice.

Why doesn't our nation have well-defined goals? Why don't we have a clear vision? Certainly it is not because those in leadership don't understand the important of goals. They know that nothing ever happens without goals. They understand that goals provide the steam in the locomotive of life. They have discovered, through their own experiences, that properly set goals — with a clear plan of action to accomplish those goals — can drive a person to overcome apparently insurmountable odds.

So why don't we have a clear national vision?

Being a visionary is costly. There is a price to be paid in order to reach goals. And few people — including our leaders — want to pay the price of pursuing real goals and big visions.

History tells us that when a national leader begins to dream dreams and see visions for his nation, he ends up paying a high price.

Mahatma Gandhi had a vision for India, and it cost him years of sacrifice and finally his life. Dr. Martin Luther King, Jr.'s most-remembered and oft-repeated sermon was his "I have a dream" speech. It became his epitaph. He was a dreamer. But his dreaming came with a price. This dream caused him many nights in the Birmingham jail. He was abused by police, ridiculed by mobs, and misunderstood by friend and foe. But it was this same dream that compelled African-Americans to stand up and take untold abuse as they fought for equality in this nation. It was this same dream that caused poor people from all races to unite and march on Washington. And — it was the same dream that cost him his life.

So you see, our nation is without a vision, dreams, or goals, because it is difficult to find men and women willing to pay the price of being dreamers. E. G. White talks about the need for such people in today's world:

> "The greatest want of the world is the want of men — men who will not be bought or sold, men who in their inmost souls are true and honest, men who do not fear to call sin by its right name, men whose conscience is as true to duty as the needle is to the pole, men who will stand for the right though the heavens fall."[1]

No man will stand for the right though the heavens fall unless he has a goal. No leader will put his neck on the line without a goal. And the people of this country will not make the sacrifice of higher taxes, cutbacks in services, and frugality on their part, until they are motivated by a clear and worthy vision.

The "Get-Rich-Quick" Philosophy

The "get-rich-quick" philosophy in this country is the second reason our nation is mired in debt. We have become a people who expect instant success. Few are willing to patiently wait for growth and success. State lotteries, casino gambling, and pyramid schemes have led many Americans to believe that wealth just happens, that wealth can be obtained without sacrifice, that success comes without effort.

In the early days of our nation, thrift, diligence, hard work, and self-denial were the prevailing values that governed wealth building. The philosophy that appears to prevail now is: Don't sacrifice—just borrow. Many seem to feel that the best way to get ahead is by using OPM—Other People's Money. In fact, in the seventies and early eighties, it was economically attractive to borrow. As the tax codes were written, you were rewarded for borrowing and penalized for saving.

Peter Wolf writes:

> "The high rates of sustained inflation experienced during the late 1970's have especially changed the mental attitude of many Americans toward savings and spending. Now, for the first time ever, saving in a bank or buying fixed-income bonds is thought to be both risky and unwise. The money saved, and the comparatively low interest earned, is understood to be eroded in actual purchasing value by the impact of inflation. On the other hand, buying tangible goods and buying on credit, as is possible with land, is thought to be safe and wise. The purchased item, it is reasoned, will only be more expensive next year. As wages and incomes continue to rise as a result of inflation, indebtedness will be repaid with 'devalued' currency. Provided the investment escalates in value along with, or at rates greater than, the rate of inflation, the asset is protected or enhanced while the debt is repaid in 'cheap dollars'. . . . Thus, inflation has induced 'buy now, pay later' thinking among individuals, corporations, and government at all levels."[2]

But what we have seen—both for individuals and the government—is that OPM has become an opiate. This philosophy of debt has become a true addiction. Our young people leave school with the idea that they must have everything now. They want and get homes, cars, clothes, vacations, and just about anything their hearts desire, without sacrifice. Unlike earlier generations that, because of tight lending policies, had to save and wait for major purchases, today's world is filled with people who must have it all now. Economists and businessmen encourage the "buy now, pay later" philosophy, because credit is seen as good fuel for an ailing economy.

What is wise for all to remember is that the only profession that starts at the top is the graveyard digger. And he began at the top because he is going down. Theo-Economics looks to the laws of nature and discovers that all growth in nature began small and grows to maturity. A cow doesn't give birth to full-grown cow. A cornstalk doesn't instantly produce a full ear of corn. How would a mother feel, if from her abdomen emerged a full-grown daughter? Just so, American citizens must be taught that the wealth of a nation and the wealth of individuals must develop in the natural order of things—from small to big. Not from big to bigger. Recapturing this sound philosophy would help curb the debt-addiction in this country. If directed by the philosophy that directs nature itself, people would see that patience does pay off. As the Hebrew scriptures say, "He that maketh haste to be rich shall not be innocent. Wealth gotten in haste shall be diminished; but he that gathereth by labor shall have increase" (Proverbs 13:11; 21:6).

Waste

Third, waste, too, keeps people and a nation in debt. We are part of the "throwaway society." One of the great dangers of affluence is the temptation to waste. We buy more, to waste more. Billions of tons of food are wasted annually. Many hours of the day are wasted by carefree, careless people. Industry creates products with obsolescence built in. Waste becomes a new industry—and also, unfortunately, a philosophy of life. Nothing has real value any more, because a replacement can always be bought.

Many of my generation grew up with the idea that waste was a sin. Our elders would quote to us many hackneyed expressions:

"Watch the pennies, and the dollars will take care of themselves."

"Haste makes waste."

"Time is money—don't waste it."

To fill your plate with food and not eat every bit of it could set off a world war. We were told that there were too many hungry people in the world to waste even a morsel of food. And too, food cost money, and few parents had the luxury of wasting money. Not that past generations didn't waste food, time, money, and other resources—because we all wasted our share. But waste wasn't built into the fabric of the economy. We understood that there was a lethal price to pay for prodigality.

Three Kinds of Waste

1. Government waste.
2. Individual waste.
3. The waste of human potential.

Government Waste

We see government waste every day and in every way. The organization called Citizens Against Government Waste provides these examples of government waste:[3]

■ $49 million for a rock-and-roll museum.

■ $15 million to Dartmouth College as part of a jobs-creation program—a total of thirty-nine jobs were created, at a cost of $324,685 each.

■ $1.36 million for preliminary work on an $18.6 million project to turn Miami Boulevard into an "exotic garden for people."

■ $566 million (rising to $900 million later in 1991) to send American cows to Europe to participate in an "Export Enhancement Program."

■ $500,000 to study the effects of cigarette smoking on dogs.

■ $107,000 to study the mating habits of Japanese quail.

■ $19 million to study whether belching by cows and other livestock harms the ozone layer.

■ $84,000 to study why people fall in love.

■ $50,000 to prove that sheepdogs do, in fact, protect sheep.

■ $46,000 to determine how long it takes to cook breakfast eggs.

■ $90,000 to study the social and behavioral aspects of vegetarianism.

■ $219,592 to teach college students how to watch television.

■ $2,500 to investigate the causes of rudeness, lying, and cheating on tennis courts.

■ $25,000 to find the best location for a new gym for the House of Representatives.

■ $2 million to renovate one of the House restaurants.

■ $350,000 to renovate the House beauty parlor.

■ $6 million to upgrade the Senate subway system.

Altogether, this concerned group found that there were some 963 social programs that added fat to the government budget. Yet waste on Capitol Hill is nothing more than a reflection of the prevailing American lifestyle. One of the reasons we don't hold the government accountable for its waste is because we enjoy the wasteful lifestyle of the government. As I was typing through this list of government waste examples, I kept asking myself, "Who asked for this money?" Somebody had to write the proposal to get it. Somebody had to come up with the idea — some private citizen, special-interest group, or perhaps a politician trying to please his constituents. Government waste is just a reflection of the American lifestyle.

Individual Waste

As mentioned earlier, we live in a throwaway society. People in this country are not concerned with frugality. Take for instance the giant leisure industry. Americans spend billions just on professional sports. It might not be so bad if they just bought tickets and watched a game. But who can watch a game without popcorn, peanuts, hot dogs, pizza, and something to drink? All wasteful junk food!

This summer, my family and I were given free tickets to a Texas Rangers (professional baseball) game. We enjoyed the game, but what fascinated me was watching people buying food, drinks, and souvenirs. I thought we were in a recession. But not from what I could observe of the people sitting in the stands. I couldn't bring myself to waste money on the junk food being hawked at the game—especially at such inflated prices. But obviously most of the spectators had no problem doing so.

Yet these are the same people who complain about government waste. These are the people who read a list like the one we shared earlier about government waste and protest. These are the ones who call loudly for a balanced government budget, even as they throw their own budgets out of balance to accommodate a wasteful lifestyle.

I believe that waste is a national epidemic. And we cannot rid ourselves of the problem by pointing fingers. We are all to blame for this national "debt addiction." Wastefulness is the American way. To stop the waste, we must begin at home. As American citizens become conscious of and committed to thrift and frugality, so will our government. Our prudence as taxpayers will result in fewer demands on the government. And fewer demands means smaller government budgets and less waste. What I am saying is that as we citizens take responsibility for our own waste, government will be forced to confront its waste as well.

The Waste of Human Potential

One of my major concerns in this book is the development of human potential. I am concerned about government and private waste, but these forms of waste are insignificant in comparison to the waste of human potential. Every person in this country has God-given talents that, if developed, could make a great difference in the economy of this country. What I have been saying in this book is that Theo-Economics calls for each person to reach his or her fullest potential. All are called on to create wealth through the development of their talents. All are responsible to God for the multiplication of their gifts. That is how an economy flourishes.

The greatest waste in a nation is not its material waste, but the waste of the God-given talents of its citizens. The business acumen of the drug dealer, the artistic ability of the graffiti scribbler, the leadership ability of an inner-city mother, the inventive mind of an assembly line worker, the wisdom and time of senior citizens (the fasting growing sector of our population), and the many other talents out there in this great land of ours — all of these have a contribution to make to society and to our economy. Our nation is suffering from debt addiction because we haven't sent the message that all citizens have the potential to produce wealth, that all citizens have the ability to make it on their own, that all citizens have a responsibility to help themselves as well as their communities.

As I travel this country presenting seminars, I am always amazed at the great potential of the people in my audiences. These people are just waiting for someone to help them tap into their potential. I would like to see us begin to speak out against the great waste of human potential in this country just as we speak out against material waste. The National Negro College Fund has a commercial that says, "The mind is a terrible thing to waste." This is true not just for African-Americans, but for every citizen of this great nation. All who read this book should take responsibility for developing their talents to the fullest and for helping others to develop theirs. Let's stop wasting human potential.

Jesus, the founder of Christianity, placed His affirmation on the virtue of frugality by commanding His disciples to gather up the fragments after He had fed the five thousand. Waste of any kind — be it time, money, food, natural resources, or human potential — costs a people dearly. Often the price is paid by re-purchasing that which has been wasted — and that with borrowed money!

It is imperative that we tackle our debt addiction in this country. We want a sound economy. Therefore we must do surgery on the things that are draining the economy. We can start dealing with this addiction by recognizing that we have a problem. We suffer, as a nation, from what in Theo-Economics, we call "The Adam Syndrome." This is when we refuse to accept the blame or responsibility for our fiscal irresponsibility. We blame the different political parties, we blame the government, we blame foreign countries, and we even blame mother nature. When the truth is—we are where we are because we choose to be there. We either didn't plan for the economic winter or knew it was coming but chose to ignore it.

A Message to the People

Your financial situation is not solely the result of outside forces. You are where you are because of the choices you have made. There is truth in the saying that you are the captain of your own financial destiny. Don't expect your ship to come in if you didn't send it out. Or if you sent your ship out on borrowed money, don't expect it to come back without strings attached to it. Debt is an addiction that will wipe you out just as certainly as AIDS. Avoid debt as you avoid AIDS. If you want to see the national debt come down, start by doing GOOD yourself.

G—Get
O—Out
O—Of
D—Debt

Don't expect the government to do what you are unwilling to do. Remember that, as the people go, so goes the nation. I believe that you and I want to and can do GOOD. Therefore, I believe our nation can eliminate this horrendous national debt.

A Message to the Government

The national debt can no longer be a political football. America's greatest resource is at stake with this spiraling deficit. Don't kill the Golden Goose. We need the golden eggs if our economy is to survive. The debt is large but not insurmountable. But modern economists cannot see any real solution. Only an economy based on "The Invisible Hand" of God can look at the financial dilemma of this country and find workable solutions. Theo-Economics is the only economy that can legitimately see possibilities in the face of apparent impossibilities.

You, the government, can do three things to remedy this critical problem:

First, create a vision for the people. We must see more than self-preserving and problem-centered actions. Show us how we can help make a better world. Design goals that will reach beyond our nation's needs. Help us see the rest of the world as our neighbors and not as our enemies. And even our enemies need to know that we will do right by them, so that even they can say we are a nation that cares. Make the vision big enough that we can sacrifice, but do not make it so big that it becomes unattainable. Remember that solving problems is not just setting goals. But setting real goals and having a real vision will solve problems.

Second, work out a balanced budget. Balance the expenses of this nation squarely with the income. Forget about economic theories that glorify deficit spending. They haven't worked. Yes, a balanced budget will hurt. But it is far less painful than a total economic collapse. We the people will bear the pain so long as the vision shows the gain.

Third, as we deal with the winter that we are now in, we dare not forget that other winters will come. The ant teaches that the only way to prepare for the winter is to save. Our nation must get back to saving. You, the government, must not only cut spending but from every budget find a way to save back a portion for rainy days. The people will rise no higher than their government. Provide a role model for us by saving, and we will begin to save. Then be sure to reward us by alleviating the taxes on saving. Taxes on saving discourage it.

The Bible tells the story of a young Israeli man who saved Egypt from a great economic winter. After revealing to Pharaoh the great famine that was to hit the country, Joseph recommended a simple

⇨   ⇨   ⇨   ⇨   ⇨   ⇨   ⇨   ⇨

economic solution—save during the years of prosperity. Pharaoh heeded his advice and saved the nation from economic ruin. Joseph was not an economist—just a foreigner God decided to use to save the nation (see Genesis 39 and 40).

No addict enjoys the withdrawal syndrome that comes when breaking free of an addiction. It is painful—sometimes even traumatic and protracted. But I have never seen an addict regret going through the pain of withdrawal when he ultimately enjoys freedom from the addiction. Theo-Economics doesn't give us the easy way. It tells us that we will go through the winter. We will experience pain, suffering, and denial. But we will be victorious.

10

Paying the Doctor Without Going Broke

While writing this book, I was brought face to face with the serious problems that exist today in health care. After my daughter's eighth-grade graduation, my wife and I thought we would run out and pick up a few groceries. On the way to the store, I was hit with sharp abdominal pains. The pains were so intense that I pulled over and gave my wife the wheel. She had driven only a few hundred yards when I cried out, "Take me to the emergency room!"

There I was diagnosed with a seven-centimeter kidney stone. The stone was so large that no treatment would move it. The pain was intense—so intense that it pushed every bit of food up and out of me. I have been told by women who have had experience with both, that kidney stones are more painful than having a baby. I can't verify that. All I know is that it hurt, and I wanted something to relieve the pain.

The nurse on duty, after struggling to get the IV in my hand, gave me a shot of some kind of anesthetic. My wife tells me that my face still showed intense pain even after the anesthetic took effect. I really don't know whether or not I was still in pain, because the drug made me completely oblivious to the world. I remember that it was not until the next morning that I began feeling the pain again. Lying there in a private hospital room, I felt the pain returning in full force.

The nurse refused to give me any more medication for pain, because I was scheduled to have a surgical treatment called lithotripsy—stone blasting. This procedure involves ultrasound waves focused directly on the stone in such force that they literally blast the stone away. I had read about this procedure several years earlier. But now I was about to experience it.

The surgery was successful, with little pain involved. But my shock came when the bills started to come in. The lithotripsy was $7,300—for an hour-and-a-half procedure! The doctor charged $2,525 for emergency care, the lithotripsy surgery, and a follow-up visit. The hospital bill, which included the emergency room visit, was $1,476. And finally, two separate lab bills came to a total of $107. The total bill for a hospital stay of about eighteen hours was $11,424! That works out to about $635 per hour. I was thankful to be free from the pain, but I was quite upset about the bill.

My family and I have had little need for medical care over the years because of good health and God's protection. Therefore, I knew nothing about the high cost of health care until this episode. I was totally shocked at the large medical bill. In fact, on my last visit to the doctor, I expressed my surprise and dismay over the bill. A bit defensive, he informed me that his charges were actually lower than those of all other doctors in the area for this particular medical procedure. He informed me that the lithotripsy—though costly—was less expensive than regular surgery for stones, which required a three- to six-day hospital stay. If the lithotripsy was less expensive, then I hated to think what the cost of removing the stones through regular surgery would be!

I still haven't gotten over the high cost of the medical care. Yet it frightens me to think of what might have happened if I had been like the 33 million people in this country who do not have medical insurance — if I had been like the millions of working people in this country who make too much money to qualify for MediCare but not enough to afford a private health care policy. This episode did help make me sensitive to the health care problem in America.

The vitality of a nation's economy is tied to the health of its people. A healthy population tends to encourage a robust economy. A nation of sick people will eventual drain the economic system. It doesn't take a genius to see that if your GNP is dependent on manpower, then what affects manpower affects the GNP.

Eighty million people make up the labor pool of this country. These are real people who have real bodies — bodies that can be affected by flu viruses, accidents on and off the job, cancer, AIDS, depression, fatigue, and many other health problems. How we help them cope with sickness will determine to a large degree how many man hours will be lost from production. So any presidential administration is wise in viewing health care as a major concern in shoring up the economy. So much rides on the well-being of working people that it is a wonder health care has just recently become a major concern in our country.

Health care is always a major concern in Theo-Economics. Because Theo-Economics always puts people before profits. It always tends the man before the machine. This prominent place of health care in Theo-Economics is owing to its view of man. Theo-Economics views man wholistically. Man has three dimensions — spiritual, mental, and physical. But man is still a unit. In order for one dimension to operate effectively, all three must operate effectively.

The gospel writer John was not an economist, but he did understand how man works. He wrote, "Beloved, I wish above all things that thou mayest prosper and be in health, even as thy soul prospereth" (3 John 2, KJV). John points out in this passage that there is an inter-relationship between health and spiritual as well as material prosperity. This wholistic view of man treats him as one unit and not three separate entities. Thus all answers to the human dilemma must take into consideration all three aspects of man.

But modern economists seem to separate these dimensions. What happens to man's psyche seems to be of no real concern to them. Health only comes into play when it begins to affect production. And spirituality seems to be viewed as having no effect at all on the workplace. Hence, the theories and formulas of modern economists are lopsided and unrealistic. In fact, that seems to be a major reason that health care in America hasn't made headlines until recently.

What has happened in this land of ours is that our labor force has grown older and more sickly, and health care costs have risen higher, with the consequent effect of draining the economy. This enormous drain has brought health care to the forefront. But since economists have never been concerned with a wholistic view of man, they have no real answer for the health care crisis in this country. People's health cannot be figured out with some logarithmic calculations. Neither can a balance sheet satisfy the hurting bodies, wrecked homes, and devastated pocketbooks of millions of Americans caught by runaway health care costs. We must find an answer to this monstrous problem, but we dare not depend solely on modern economists.

I must confess that this is a difficult chapter to write. There are no easy answers to the health care crisis. Health care involves ethics as well as economics. It involves machines as well as men. It requires restrictions while trying to keep freedoms. It is concerned with community while seeking to meet the needs of the individual. As I look at the many faces of health care, no one person is adequate to address such a complex issue. So I will not try to give a panacea for this mega-problem. What I will do is simply relate health care to the basic theme we have been looking at in Theo-Economics — the theme of responsibility.

Looking at health care from my vantage point, I believe that calling the different entities of health care to genuine responsibility would go farther in remedying this problem — with more long-term positive effects and better health for the American people — than perhaps any other single suggestion. You see, health care, unlike any other area of economics, is largely driven by the decisions people make, along with their lifestyles.

It is not a mystery as to why heart disease is the leading cause of death in America. It has little to do with people having access to health care. It is about the daily diet and exercise choices of the American people. It is about the high-stress lives of people caught up in materialism, trying to "keep up with the Joneses." It is about a nation more concerned with success than good health. The call to personal responsibility puts health care issues right in the laps of the people who can do something about it.

In this book, I bring us back again and again to personal responsibility. Theo-Economics does not allow man to shift his responsibility to others. "Every tub must sit on its own bottom." Every adult citizen is accountable for his or her own actions. We seem to have forgotten about that in today's world. We want to hold everyone else responsible for our actions. Health care in this country is viewed as a governmental problem and not as a personal problem. We are a sick nation because of what the government has or hasn't done — or so many believe. But is that really the case? When I look at the irresponsibility of the average citizen when it comes to health in this country, I am amazed that there are any well people at all. The preservation of this nation's intemperate masses is one of the convicting points of Theo-Economics. If God were not involved in the world, we would all have died long ago from the effects of our indulgent lifestyles.

The typical American diet of meat and potatoes is enough to keep people stopped up and ripe for colon cancer. The kidneys of the average U.S. citizen should have exploded by now from the millions of soft drinks consumed each year. We experience far too much limb amputation, blindness, and death from diabetes caused by the large consumption of refined sugar. It is a wonder we don't have many more job-related accidents and defective products due to the loss of brain cells destroyed by the oceans of alcoholic beverages we pour into ourselves after work. It is a mystery that our workforce has not gone up completely in the stale, cancerous smoke of cigarettes.

Yet we charge the government with the health crisis in this

country. Wake up, America! Resolving the health care problem in this country must begin with us. The long-term answer to health care is preventive medicine, not protective insurance. And preventive medicine begins with the individual.

In the very beginning, God gave directives for proper health care. "Then God said, I give you every seed-bearing plant on the face of the whole earth and every tree that has fruit with seed in it. They will be your food" (Genesis 1:29). He placed man on a strict vegetarian diet and promised spiritual, physical, and financial prosperity to all its adherents. Hundreds of years later, God repeated His dietary laws—along with sanitary, civic, and moral laws—with this curse:

> "If you do not carefully follow all the words of this law, which are written in this book, and do not revere this glorious and awesome name—the Lord your God—the Lord will send fearful plagues on you and your descendants, harsh and prolonged disaster, and severe and lingering illnesses. He will bring upon you all the diseases of Egypt that you dreaded, and they will cling to you. The Lord will bring on you every kind of sickness and disaster not recorded in this Book of the Law, until you are destroyed" (Deuteronomy 28:58-60).

In other words, God was saying, I have given you instruction on how to live a healthy life, but you must take responsibility to obey the instructions. Theo-Economics accepts God's call to responsibility for healthful living. Five levels of health care are a part of this call to responsibility. They are:

1. Personal responsibility.
2. Physician responsibility.
3. Community responsibility.
4. Health care provider responsibility.
5. Governmental responsibility.

Personal Responsibility

The ground floor of health care is the individual citizen. All other levels of health care are in direct response to the individual's personal responsibility for his or her health. Therefore this call to responsibility must begin with individuals.

Unquestionably, we must expect more accountability on the part of the citizens of this country. We can no longer allow the people of this great land of ours to think that the answer to the health care crisis is solely the responsibility of the government, politicians, or economists. We must see that resolving the health care crisis begins with us taking care of our own health. The four major killers in this country are:

1. Heart disease.
2. Cancer.
3. Stroke.
4. Diabetes.

Scientific data have confirmed in recent years that every one of these killers is linked directly to lifestyle choices, including dietary habits. Americans have become more health conscious in the last dozen or more years. But studies show that this consciousness about health is limited primarily to the more affluent. It is ironic that those who can most afford health care are the ones who take more responsibility for their health and thus need health care less.

As for the general public, it seems that many manage their health like they manage their money—poorly. It seems that many don't see the correlation between managing their health and the health care crisis in this country. If the general public were to become concerned about their own health, we would see a drastic drop in the demand for health care services. We would have a far healthier populace.

To get the masses to become more responsible for their health, we should spend more time educating people about the prevention of diseases. This would also mean a change of health care philosophy in this country. We would move from crisis intervention—a disease-cure approach—to a wholistic approach to medicine. Walter E. Wiset, in the book, *Health Care and Its Costs—a Challenge for the Church*, describes wholistic medicine:

> "It is a medical system built fundamentally on health care rather than disease-cure. It appreciates the need for (and it uses) sophisticated high-tech medicine for crisis interventions. More

basically, however, it prizes health maintenance and disease prevention.

"It views health as a positive state of being, not simply as the absence of disease.

"It addresses persons in their physical, mental, emotional, spiritual dimensions — all dimensions of one unified self. It addresses persons in their social and physical environments, environments which are part of their health or disease.

"It avoids the 'spare parts mentality' that has begun to invade modern medicine, particularly in shaping attitudes toward organ transplantation.

"It attempts to empower persons to participate in their own healing and responsibility to maintain their own health.

"It uses approaches which mobilize the person's own capacities for self-healing."[1]

Wholistic medicine calls people to responsibility. It encourages them to practice preventive medicine. It tells them that "an ounce of prevention is better than a pound of cure." It is more concerned with teaching them how to live healthier lives than with just telling them how to gain access to health care facilities. It shares with them the eight essential for good health, which are as follows:

1. Proper diet. This includes a balanced diet of grains, fruits, nuts, and vegetables in proper combinations and properly prepared; regulated times for eating; the amount and manner of eating (eating slowly and never overeating); and a cheerful attitude while eating.

2. Exercise. We are in the midst of a fitness boom in this country. But this physical fitness fad has become perhaps too closely identified with affluence. It often doesn't push wellness for the sake of health but for the sake of status. Many people probably feel that they can't exercise unless they have the proper exercise outfit and membership at the local health club. But fitness and science experts all agree that walking is still the best exercise. And you can do that for free. You don't even need a special outfit.

3. Water. We should be thankful to live in a land where there is an abundance of clean water. We human beings need at least eight glasses of water a day. Plus, we need water to wash the impurities off the skin by daily baths.

4. Sunshine. Every day we should soak up the sun's rays. Spending time in the sunshine allows us to draw in much-needed vitamin D. But beware — extended periods of sunbathing can be dangerous to the skin, leading in time to skin cancer.

5. Fresh air. No one can survive without air. We know and understand its importance. Getting sufficient fresh air means spending some time each day in the out-of-doors inhaling deeply. Many spend all day in windowless buildings breathing recycled air. Therefore, it is essential that at least our homes be ventilated with fresh air.

6. Sleep. Every person needs a minimum of eight hours of sleep each night. The body needs time to rest and recharge. Studies have shown that people who get eight hours of sleep stay healthier and are far more productive.

7. Proper attitude. The large majority of illnesses in America are psychosomatic. Psychosomatic illnesses are those brought on by mental problems such as anxiety, depression, or stress. Theo-Economics suggests adherence to the words of God:

> "Do not be anxious about anything, but in everything by prayer and petitions, with thanksgiving, present your request to God. And the peace of God, which transcends all understanding, will guard your hearts and your mind in Christ Jesus. Finally, brothers, whatever is true, whatever is noble, whatever is right, whatever is pure, whatever is lovely, whatever is admirable — if anything is excellent or praiseworthy — think on such things" (Philippians 4:6-8).

8. Trust in God. This is the capstone of sound health, but I will expound further on this subject in the final chapter — "In God We Trust."

Preventive medicine, as described above, allows people to experience better health, which in turn reduces their need to use health care professionals and facilities. Education of the general public on general health care and preventive medicine will go a long way in helping to keep health care costs down.

Physician Responsibility

Doctors play a critical part in solving the health care crisis in this country. The kind and cost of care doctors give their patients is a large factor in the health care equation. But some believe that doctors need not be called to responsibility — that they are not part of the problem. In fact, it seems that many doctors themselves feel that they are not part of the problem. After years of medical school, often at the sacrifice of family, friends, and a relationship with God, they believe that whatever they can obtain, they deserve. I personally know quite a few doctors, and I don't envy their rigorous training or their long working hours. But that by no means excuses them from taking responsibility for the part they play in this health care crisis.

In Theo-Economics we are constantly reminded that men are sinful human beings — and that includes the medical doctors. All men are capable of falling prey to greed, neglect, and mismanagement. Doctors, like all other American citizens, need to be held accountable for their actions. There are three areas in which I believe physicians need to take more responsibility:

Personal finance. Doctors are no better at handling their money than the general public. They spend years in school learning how to heal people, but little if any time learning how to manage their money. On finishing medical school, they become ripe victims for the "buy-now, pay-later" philosophy. Banks consider doctors excellent credit risks and therefore make it easy for them to obtain loans to help them settle into their practices. With huge school loans, high home mortgages, and other loans as they begin their practices, doctors typically start out with a ton of debt. The huge debt servicing and poor management of money keeps doctors on the brink of financial disaster, which in turn affects the cost of practice.

Sitting next to me on a plane was a doctor. We began talking and discovered we had similar interests. We both were interested in helping people manage their money better. In fact, we both were enroute to a destination where we each were to present different seminars on money management. I was going to instruct a church group, and he, a group of doctors.

"I thought doctors didn't have money problems," I said.

He chuckled, then replied, "Most of my friends make up to $500,000 a year, but at the end of each month, they are broke. They have problems living within budgets, don't know how to collect on insurance, and don't know how to manage the office help. All of this keeps doctors in financial problems."

What a sad commentary! And the losers, in part, are the patients, who end up paying for their doctors' mismanagement in higher fees. Of course, not all doctors are poor money managers, but based on on the personal debt and management of the average American, the number who are is a lot higher than we would like to think. Higher education doesn't make you a better money manager. What makes you a better money manager is taking responsibility for your own personal finance. If doctors were to free themselves from so much debt (including large home mortgages) and begin managing their money more wisely, they could lower their fees and make a serious dent in the health care crisis.

Competition, as mentioned before, is destructive to any system. And competition to become the best and most affluent doctor is costing us an arm and a leg. Now, I have no problem with doctors making money, because they do provide an important service. But I do have a problem with doctors who seem only to be concerned with living the "Lifestyles of the Rich and Famous." Some doctors seem to be in a race to see who can live in the biggest house, have the biggest practice, make the most money, and take the most exotic vacations. There seems to be no concern about proper stewardship among such doctors.

Most doctors don't start out this way, but the competition draws too many of them in. If you are going to be out in front, you will have to live in a certain neighborhood, drive a certain car, take out a membership in a certain country club, send your children to private preparatory schools—and the list never ends. Before long, a doctor can become caught up in a conspicuous, consumptive lifestyle that affects the cost of health care.

I make a plea to doctors. Stop allowing others to dictate your life. Live within your means. Set a ceiling on your spending and limits on your lifestyle. Just because you make good money, you are not under obligation to spend it all on yourself. Read again Chapter 5, on the purpose of wealth. Then remember that you are in a profession where you gain your wealth from the misfortunes of others. There is no sin in profiting from helping sick people. The sin is in mismanaging and misusing the money made from people's misfortunes.

The lure of greed. Doctors must fight the temptation of greed. Physicians are no different than anyone else in society. They too have fallen prey to the greed that has run rampant in today's world. Wealth is alluring, and the more one makes, the more one wants. To deny this temptation is to deny the sinful nature of man. We do have good doctors, but even the good doctors—if they don't stay on guard—will get sucked into a vortex of greed. No one is immune to the temptation of greed. The call to responsibility is a call to recognize this danger as well as to take control of one's life.

Community Responsibility

Solving the health care problem will take the joint effort of many people. Individuals and doctors must do their part. The government also has a part to play. But communities as well must begin taking responsibility for health care.

Communities must do as they have done in addressing the problem of crime. They must form watch groups that monitor the health of individuals and health care facilities in their area. Theo-Economics would call that being your brother's keeper. We can no longer live isolated lives apart from our neighbors. We don't need nosey people, but we do need caring, concerned people who will watch out for one another's health. These community-based health-watch groups can monitor community clinics and doctors to insure accountability from both. Then the community can help drive down the cost of malpractice insurance by looking for others ways to settle health claims than by extravagant lawsuits. I have doctor friends who have left the profession because of the high cost of malpractice insurance and the constant fear of being sued. These are good people who could not bear alone the full cost burden of being in business. The community does have a vital part to play in health care.

Health Care Provider Responsibility

Another big factor in the health care equation is health care providers. Hospitals, clinics, and health maintenance organizations are all part of the health care puzzle. The struggles and challenges are the same for health care providers as for doctors. Greed, competition, and mismanagement have sent costs through the ceiling. It seems that everyone wants to deny a reality that has swept through every part of our society.

The eighties were years of business take-overs, junk bonds, and scandals from the White House to God's House. And even though the medical profession hasn't received the same media scrutiny as many others have, the sin of greed has nonetheless been sighted in its midst. The huge debts many hospitals carry because of their ever-expanding facilities and high-tech medical equipment ependitures, along with the enormous salaries of hospital executives, all add to the high cost of health care in America. But again, no one wants to take responsibility. It is all too easy to cast the blame at someone else's door. Our only hope for settling the health care crisis in this country is for all entities to take responsibility.

Governmental Responsibility

Finally, the government has a role to play in solving this major American problem. It must be understood from the beginning that the government can never solve the health care crisis alone. I emphasize that, because many expect the government to wave a magic wand and fix the problem. Sometimes it appears that even the government itself feels it must play God in solving the health care crisis. Because of the sheer size of the problem, the government must take a leadership role, but we must never see it as the panacea for all the nation's woes—and that includes health care.

In Theo-Economics, we would call that idolatry. The government is ordained by God to protect and care for its citizens, but not to act in the place of God. Theo-Economics teaches people that the government is to be held responsible for its specific functions, but that ultimate responsibility rests with God. So we may turn to the government to help resolve some problems but know that God intervenes and does the resolving.

The government's job is to continue to write and enforce legislation that will protect American citizens from charlatan doctors, rip-off insurance companies, medical monopolies, and unhealthy and unsafe consumer products — but never to guarantee the health of its people. True health care is an individual responsibility.

We can never call for a health safety net for the American people. As moves are afoot to create a national health insurance, we must be mindful never to take away responsibility. Health insurance is not health assurance. If we do not answer the call to responsibility at the different levels of health care in this country, health care will become a health crunch.

A national health insurance can be a boon for the many citizens locked out of health care, provided those citizens do not see the insurance as guaranteeing good health. Good health comes from taking responsibility for one's life. Preventive medicine is the best way to pay the doctor without going broke. Doctors and health care providers will be needed far less, thus dramatically reducing costs for the patient and the country.

11

I Love to Pay My Taxes

Is this a joke? No! Neither is this just an attention getter. I really believe, based on my study of Theo-Economics, that taxes should never cause anxiety. April 15 of each year should be a time of thankfulness for all United States citizens. But for most people, April 15 is "D-day." The negative attitudes that fill this land about taxes are almost enough in themselves to destroy any economy.

Several reasons exist for the negative attitudes about taxation in America. One is our lack of appreciation for the role and place of government in society. Another is our lack of information about the use of taxes. And finally, the misuse of tax dollars by the government. Let's look at these three reasons that hinder us from saying, "I Love to Pay My Taxes."

For the average citizen, when the word *government* is mentioned, red flags pop up. The government is seen as the enemy. And if not the enemy, then no better than a necessary evil. In a free society like America, the question is asked, Why do we even need a government? We can govern ourselves.

Theo-Economics clarifies the place of government in society. It starts by showing the legitimacy of the government.

> "Everyone must submit himself to the governing authority, for there is no authority except that which God has established. The authorities that exist have been established by God" (Romans 13:1, 2).

So the government is not the bad guy. It is ordained by God to carry out a specific function. Theo-Economics operates on the basis that after mankind sinned, it became difficult for people to live in harmony with each other. Our natural inclination since the entrance of sin to the planet is to oppress, covet, and to grasp after power, property, and possessions. Therefore, God has appointed a referee to keep man from destroying himself. The function of the government, as ordained by God, is to maintain order among men. Since it has divine authority, God expects us to give due respect and honor to it. "Therefore, it is necessary to submit to the authorities, not only because of possible punishment, but also because of conscience. This is also why you pay taxes" (Romans 13:5, 6).

In order to keep a government intact, it must be funded. And since government is a service, not an industry, tax dollars are needed to fund it. This concept of a divinely ordained government ought to make it easier for us to pay our taxes. Since the government is God-ordained, God holds Himself responsible for its actions. Men need not fret, because this "Invisible Hand" will interpose Himself to rectify all ills. Biblical history testifies to God's intervention into governmental affairs in order to correct its abuses. I love to pay my taxes, because I know that government is ordained of God to carry on its function of maintaining order and justice — and that God will always be in control.

Interesting, isn't it, that we taxpayers often complain about taxes but seldom about the benefits we derive from those taxes? The way most taxpayers kick about taxes, it's as if there were no positive benefits. But even a surface view of the advantages received from paying taxes would cause many to stop their murmuring and complaining.

Working on this book has made me even more aware of the

blessings associated with a broad tax base such as we have in this country. Recently, on a short driving trip, I crossed literally dozens of bridges. Many of them I didn't even notice until I had gone over them. When you think of the many bodies of water that separate lands, bridges become vitally important. Without bridges, travel would be extremely difficult and in some places impossible. The many thousands of bridges that serve to connect lands across this country were paid for in large part by tax dollars. "I love to pay my taxes," because I love to travel this beautiful, majestic country, and bridges help make that possible.

"You don't miss the water until the well runs dry" is an old saying that reflects how easy it is to take for granted the blessings all around us. In this country, we are privileged to have millions of miles of paved, scenic country roads, convenient state highways, and wide interstate freeways—all paid for by tax dollars. In the majority of homes, we have the luxury of pure, clean water—both hot and cold—available at the twist of a faucet. We have seen contagious diseases almost completely wiped out because of the excellent sanitary systems of this country. Even though our cities struggle with crime, just think how it would be if there were no paid policemen. I can imagine it would be like the old wild west. And the homes we cherish so much—could we afford to protect them from fire with our own personal fire department?

The list of benefits from taxes goes on and on. But I believe you get the point. "I love to pay my taxes," because I like to take hot baths. I like the convenience of turning up a thermostat for heat instead of chopping wood or hauling coal. I appreciate the complex phone systems, the modern airports, the educational opportunities—so when tax time comes, I pay my taxes with thankfulness.

Now, please don't get me wrong. I am not naive. Neither am I blind. I am well aware of the abuses in our tax system—the billions of dollars wasted each year by politicians and government, the inequities in the distribution of the tax burden, and the thousands of loopholes that the well-informed wiggle through to trim their tax bills. These things evoke legitimate complaints and concerns. But even with all the abuses, our taxes aren't heavy compared to their benefits.

I am not encouraging or calling for more taxes. I just want us to be fair with ourselves. Americans still flock to the stadiums to watch sporting events. Our homes are filled with labor-saving devices and many other gadgets we don't even need. We crowd the amusements parks and fill our stomachs at the concession stands. And then we have the nerve to complain about taxes. If in fact the taxes in this country were as heavy as we make them appear, many of the things just mentioned would have to go. Taxes aren't what we want them to be, but they surely aren't what we have made them out to be, either.

I believe that the biggest bear in the whole tax controversy is me — the average taxpayer. I believe you and I do more damage to ourselves than does the IRS. What Theo-Economics teaches us is that we are responsible, to a large degree, for our own destiny. Jesus the Nazarene lived during a time when taxes were extremely heavy. The Jews in His day had to pay taxes both to the local temple and to the Roman government. They were constantly complaining about their taxes.

One day they sought to draw Jesus into a debate over the tax issue. Jesus simply replied, "Give to Caesar what is Caesar's, and to God what is God's" (Matthew 22:21). He understood all about the tax burden and the abuse. But He also understood that it takes more energy to fret over the taxes than it does to create more wealth to pay the taxes. In fact, on yet another occasion, Jesus was questioned by one of His own disciples about paying taxes. Peter was anxious, because church officials were inquiring about Jesus' tax bill. On querying Jesus about the taxes, Peter received this command: "Go to the lake and throw out your line. Take the first fish you catch; open its mouth and you will find a four-drachma coin. Take it and give it to them for my tax and yours" (Matthew 17:27).

Using Jesus as a model, Theo-Economics concludes that haggling over taxes is wasted time and energy — that we would do better for ourselves and the government to spend more time creating wealth than in fighting over taxes.

Loving to pay our taxes does not mean that we never speak

out against tax abuses. It does not mean that we sit idly by while taxes go through the ceiling. We as citizens are under moral obligation to hold the government accountable for the use of taxes. But when we call for accountability on the part of the government, it must not be selfishly motivated. We must be concerned with justice and efficiency, not with demanding less tax so we can waste more.

Theo-Economists believe that the use of taxes by the government should be limited. The government can never be the complete answer to the needs of a country. The responsibility of the nation must be shared by everyone. Therefore, the use of taxes should be limited to providing for major services and needs of the country. It should cover the operational expenses of the government.

But the government should not use tax dollars as a means of stimulating the economy. What the government does in providing services and protecting its citizens does affect the economy. But it should not be the plan of the government to spend as a means of righting the economy. This kind of policy leads to deficit spending, which leads to disaster. Any increase in taxes should be based primarily on providing services and protection for the people of the country.

Stimulating or manipulating the economy is extremely volatile and risky. The government is God-ordained but it is not God. Fixing the economy, as we have seen demonstrated in recent years, is beyond the scope of man. Therefore, Theo-Economics sees that divine intervention is the only sure answer to a broken economy. ⇨ ⇨ ⇨ ⇨ ⇨ ⇨ ⇨ ⇨

Message to the Government

We the taxpayers are happy to pay our taxes, because we appreciate the services rendered by local, state, and federal government. But never take our contentment as cowardliness or passivity. We still hold you accountable for fairness, frugality, faithfulness, and justice. We believe it our patriotic and moral duty to cry out against excesses, abuses, and injustices. Therefore, you can count on us to vote our convictions. You can count on us to ask questions and expect honest answers. We love our country. Therefore we expect you to work hard to see to it that our country is operated in as efficient and effective a manner as possible.

Message to the Taxpayer

Stop looking at taxes as a burden. Consider it a privilege and a blessing to be able to pay taxes. Remember that paying taxes, for the most part, means you have a job or have created a job. It takes less energy to create more wealth to pay more taxes than it does to worry or haggle over paying them. Spend your time thinking of creative ways to earn more money. This helps you as well as the nation. The more wealth you create, the better off the nation.

Think differently. If you want less taxes, begin your own campaign to encourage Americans to demand less from the government. We cannot demand the latest in technology and a high standard of living without expecting to pay the bill. There is no free lunch. Remember that the government doesn't create wealth—it only uses it. The only money the government has is what we give it.

12

In God We Trust

What makes a sound foundation for an economy? Is it gold, silver, abundant natural resources, manufacturing tools and facilities? Is it something tangible? Many would choose one if not all of these things, believing them to be part of a solid foundation for any economy. But on closer examination, we discover that though gold, silver, natural resources, and manufacturing tools and facilities play an important role in an economy, they do not provide a solid foundation for it.

In the construction industry, the foundation is the most important part of the building. Any good building contractor will tell you that you may cut corners on any other part of the building and perhaps get away with it. But you will always pay dearly for short-changing on the foundation. It is the part of the structure that carries the entire weight of the building. It is the base upon which all other building materials stand. Therefore, the foundation is generally the most costly part of building, as well as the one of most concern to a good contractor.

The same holds true for an economy. The foundation of any

159

economy will determine its success. Our founding fathers were well aware of this. So they thought long and hard before digging the footings and putting down the foundation of our economy. The natural resources of America are immense, but the founding fathers didn't think them enough on which to build the nation's economy. Our nation is a leader in manufacturing tools and facilities, but these were never considered seriously by our founding fathers as the base for our economy. They were wise in perceiving that it is not tangible things that ground an economy. As they studied the history of nations and human behavior, they were convinced that what anchors economics is relationships. And what cements relationships is trust.

This intangible quality called trust cannot be qualified or quantified and is not predictable; therefore, modern economists are hesitant to point to trust as the foundation of today's economy. But it was the unpredictable nature of humans and human systems that caused the founding fathers to look for the intangible to solidify the economy.

Their search ended with God. Boldly engraved on every piece of American money are the words, "In God We Trust." God became the foundation of the American economy. The patriarchs could find no better foundation on which to build.

Why would the founding fathers of this nation incorporate such pregnant words into the monetary system? Couldn't they have found something better to put their trust in? Background research on some of the more prominent founding fathers reveals that all of them exercised a strong belief in God. Men like Benjamin Franklin, Thomas Jefferson, John and Jay Adams, George Washington, and others were students of the Bible. Many of these men were not ashamed or afraid to confess their belief in God.

In fact, as they studied human history and worked to better the world's conditions, they were convinced that there had to be an invisible force at work in the affairs of men. They were well aware that occurrences in this world, including the establishment of this country, were not by accident or human design. They knew well their human limitations. And since they had not been spoiled by the scientific discoveries of today, it was far easier for them to factor God into their reasoning. To them it was logical to see a universal God behind the affairs of man. The world was too complex and situations too grave to think that man alone could solve them or that chance and time would heal all ills.

The founding fathers accepted the Bible as God's Word. They saw in it sound principles to govern man here on earth as well as for eternity. In fact, all the Ivy League universities of today started out as religious institutions. The Bible was the bedrock of their curriculum. Some of the founding fathers attended these Ivy League schools and spent as much as three hours a day studying the Bible. And even those who did not attend the universities were certainly influenced by Bible teaching, which was a part of the fabric of seventeenth-century thinking. Their understanding of God was shaped by the Old Testament prophet's words:

> "Do you not know? Have you not heard? Has it not been told you from the beginning? Have you not understood since the earth was founded? He sits enthroned above the circle of the earth and its people are like grasshoppers. He stretches out the heavens like a canopy and spreads them out like a tent to live in. He brings princes to naught and reduces the rulers of this world to nothing. No sooner are they sown, no sooner do they take root in the ground than he blows on them and they wither, and a whirlwind sweeps them away like chaff. To whom will you compare me? Or who is my equal? says the Holy One. Lift your eyes and look at the heavens. Who created all these? He who brings out the starry host one by one, and calls them each by name. Because of his great power and mighty strength, not one of them is missing (Isaiah 40:21-26).

Scriptures such as this and many others convinced the patriarchs that an omnipotent, omniscient, and omnipresent God must be the bedrock of the nation's economy.

"In God We Trust" is laced with powerful implications. By writing "In God We Trust" on every denomination of American money, the founding fathers made a corporate statement. The personal pronoun *we* announces that there was a consensus among the leaders of this country about God's involvement in the affairs of man. And it can be deduced by the acceptance of the general public that they too were in agreement with such a broad, sweeping declaration. Men saw and experienced the "Invisible Hand" in the economy and were willing to acknowledge God's immanence.

Implied also in this pregnant proclamation is the concept of relationship. Relationship is built on trust, and trust can only accrue between persons. Thus God was viewed by our founding fathers as a personal God. He was seen as an approachable divine being concerned with His creatures.

These architects of the American economy believed in the Creator-creature relationship. It was part of their understanding that "God created man in his own image, in the image of God created he him; male and female created he them" (Genesis 1:27, KJV). They were not confused about man's origins. Since God is man's Creator, these early pioneers believed that God obligated Himself to take care of man. They believed God to be active in all of human life. They were convinced that He was Someone worthy of their trust.

Trusting is a deep concept. Trusting implies explicit confidence. It means relying on the integrity, veracity, justice, and friendship or sound principles of another. So for Benjamin Franklin, Thomas Jefferson, and the others, God was more than just an intellectual concept. He was a divine being who could be known, worshiped, and relied on. Trusting means that God was and is willing to let Himself be known to man. These patriotic men testified — in this dauntless declaration, "In God We Trust" — that they had come to know this personal God. How can you say you trust someone if you don't know Him? These men knew Him and found that He could be trusted.

Trusting God is good for spiritual growth, but is trusting God sound economics? Many in today's world don't think so. "What has God to do with it?" is the question raised by modern economists. Others assert that business and religion don't mix. But what we must understand is that God transcends religion. The concept of God moves beyond denominational borders. Before there were denominations, there was God. The founding fathers understood this. They accepted the universality of

God. They were careful, though, to identify God as the only true God of the Bible. He was not just a higher power — not just the greatest God among many gods. He was the only God. "Hear, O Israel: the Lord our God is one" (Deuteronomy 6:4).

The men who wrote the constitution and set the economic cornerstone of this country came out of the great reformation tradition. They held to monotheism — the belief in one God. Thus they could believe that the earth was not only created by God but held together by God. They believed that God is the owner of everything, having placed man in the position of manager. If in fact God is the owner, then it would hold true that nothing can go on without His consent or permission. In other words, all human activity is affected by God. Hence, any economy that attempts to function without God is attempting an impossible feat.

The New Testament gospel writer quotes Jesus as saying, "Apart from me [God] you can do nothing" (John 15:5). Is trusting God sound economics? The world belongs to God, proclaim the psalms. The prophet Haggai writes, "The silver is mine and the gold is mine, declares the Lord Almighty" (Haggai 2:8). If God owns everything, then that makes Him the bank and the banker. Wouldn't it be sound economics to have both the bank and the banker in our corner? The pioneers of this nation thought so and engraved their belief on every governmental medium of exchange.

"In God We Trust" also implied the accountability of man to God. There is reciprocity in a trusting relationship. God can be expected to intervene in man's economy, but God does expect obedience from man. The founding fathers believed that all of their economic decisions must pass the scrutiny of God and His Word. God is the owner of everything. We are His stewards — His managers. Good stewardship demands strict obedience. America's patriarchs comprehended the parallel between biblical stewardship and a sound economy. "So then, men ought to regard us as servants of Christ and as those entrusted with the secret things of God. Now it is required that those who have been given a trust must prove faithful" (1 Corinthians 4:1, 2). The Greek in this biblical reference for the phase "those entrusted" means "house manager" or "steward." The Greek word used in the phase "those entrusted" is *oikonomous*. This word is the root word for our English word *economy*. In this scriptural passage God declares that some things are beyond human wisdom — they are secret things. And yet this relationship between God and man allows Him to entrust man with secret information. As man trusts God, so God trusts man with hidden information on how to manage earth's resources. He gives men this clandestine wisdom according to their trustworthiness. And as long as they use this classified information for the betterment of society, God continues to reveal more to men. Our founding fathers knew that they did not have the wisdom to answer the complexities of a growing nation and a growing economy, so they gladly acknowledged themselves as simply stewards of God's world. They looked to God for the wisdom to direct the nation and its economy.

America's money still declares that we trust in God. But does what we engrave on our money testify to what is really in our hearts? It appears that trusting God is at a very low level in this land of ours. We have placed our trust in military weapons — which is why it is so difficult to trim the military budget. We look to scholars to work out answers to our many complex economic problems. Our textbooks are filled with theories that never seek the hidden wisdom of God. Yet boldly emblazoned on both our paper and coined money are the words, "In God We Trust."

Now, please, don't get me wrong. I am glad to see that God is still in the thinking of America, even if only at a subconscious level. What concerns me is that what has always grounded the economy is slipping away from us. And we would do well to move back to trusting God. I do believe it is cheaper and more sound.

Why has our motherland moved away from this dependence on God? We live in time when men — through logic, reason, and scientific discovery — have found answers to many inexplicable complexities. Science has taken us to the very edge of human discovery. Mathematical computations whizzed out by high-powered computers have brought findings heretofore beyond the scope of man within our reach. We have smashed the atom, thought for centuries to be indivisible, and discovered sub-atomic particles. With this kind of scientific know-how, why do we need God? Many believe that with enough time and information, we can discover all that needs to be discovered for man's prosperity on Planet Earth.

But both scientists and economists must confess that though man can analyze, diagnose, and tear apart, he has been unable to fix the world. Scientists can split sub-atomic particles, but they will never discover the right recipe to put those particles back together to create life. Economists will continue to write econometric theories, but they will never know what is in the heart of man.

And what is in the heart of man is what affects the economy. Economists call it consumer confidence—just a nice way of describing the unpredictable ways of human beings. Only God knows what is in the heart of man.

> "The heart of man is deceitful above all things and beyond cure. Who can understand it? I the Lord search the heart and examine the mind, to reward a man according to his conduct, according to what his deeds deserve" (Jeremiah 17:9, 10).

The sculptors of the American constitution and economic system understood well that they could not put their trust in man or materials—and they chose to put their trust in God. They knew what we must come to know again as a nation:

> "This is what the Lord says: Cursed is the one who trusts in man, who depends on flesh for his strength and whose heart turns away from the Lord. He will be like a bush in the wastelands, he will not see prosperity when it comes. He will dwell in the parched places of the desert, in a salt land where no one lives" (Jeremiah 17:5, 6).

The founding fathers saw the wisdom of grounding our economy in God. They were convinced that trusting God was sound economic planning. "But blessed is the man who trusts in the Lord, whose confidence is in him. He will be like a tree planted by the water that sends out its roots by the stream. It does not fear when heat comes; its leaves are always green, it has no worries in a year of drought and never fails to bear fruit" (Jeremiah 17: 7, 8). No wonder the forefathers of this country were so optimistic about its prosperity. They had a sure foundation for the economy: "In God We Trust." Indeed, in God they trusted.

Conclusion

I did not write this book with the idea of presenting all the right answers about all the economic problems of this nation—or any other nation. What I have first tried to do is to bring into focus God's place in any economy, along with man's responsibility. Also, I've tried to show that there is another economy (Theo-Economics) that operates above and through all human economies.

Let me now offer some suggestions on what to do with the material in this book.

First, weigh everything you have read in this book. Go back through each chapter and tear it apart, bit by bit. Disagree with my conclusions—or find out how you agree. Then sit down and write me a letter expressing your discoveries. I want to hear from you.

Second, find some friends with whom to share this book. Begin discussion groups about the book and other economic issues. In your groups, don't spend time talking just about the problems but work toward your own solutions. Remember that God can use you, as He did Joseph, to provide answers to our economic problems.

Third, it is important that you continue your own personal search for God's answers to economic concerns. This means that you will need to increase your personal knowledge of the Bible, since the Bible is God's manual for understanding Theo-Economics.

167

Fourth, start taking responsibility for your own financial destiny. Begin living on a budget. Avoid debt. Be aware of waste. Take care of your health. And deepen your trust in God. Once you begin living in God's economy, you will become convinced — as I have — that your financial well being is not tied to human economic conditions.

Fifth, as mentioned earlier, attitude does determine altitude. What you think and believe determines, to a large degree, where you will end up. Currently most talk about the economy, whether personal or corporate, is negative. And I am quick to admit that, through the lens of human economy, the picture isn't so bright. But what I have done in this book is to give you another pair of glasses through which to look at the economy.

You can now see the economy through the eyes of God. You can now look at modern economic systems and see God's economy — Theo-Economics — in operation. This new view will allow you to be positive about the final outcomes both of our nation's economy and your own personal finances.

The apostle Paul writes in the manual (Bible) for Theo-Economics:

> "Do not be anxious about anything, but in everything, by prayer and petition, with thanksgiving, present your request to God. And the peace of God, which transcends all understanding, will guard your hearts and your minds in Christ Jesus. Finally, brothers, whatever is true, whatever is noble, whatever is right, whatever is pure, whatever is lovely, whatever is admirable — if anything is excellent or praiseworthy — think about such things" (Philippians 4:6-8).

The future wasn't so bright for Paul as he wrote these words. He was facing death while chained in a dark, damp prison cell in Rome. But he had learned years earlier that it is not where you are or what you have that determines your ultimate outcome. That is determined by your outlook. Paul continues:

> "I know what it is to be in need, and I know what it is to have plenty. I have learned the secret of being content in any and every situation, whether well fed or hungry, whether living in

plenty or in want. I can do everything through him [Jesus Christ] who gives me strength" (Philippians 4:11-13).

Paul understood that, even though we must live in human economies, we don't have to be trapped by them. God does have His own economy for those who choose to live in it. In this new economy, there is no fear, frustration, or failure. Instead, there is peace, calm, and security, because this economic system has God as its foundation. Paul's final words are these: "And my God will meet all our needs according to his glorious riches in Christ Jesus" (Philippians 4:19).

What a positive outlook! No other economic system can make such an economic forecast and promise.

About the Author

Dr. Roland J. Hill is president of the Financial Freedom Foundation, a nonprofit organization committed to teaching Theo-Economics. This ministry seeks to help the unemployed, the under-employed, and all who want to maximize their God-given gifts and talents to help themselves, others, and the Kingdom of God. If you would like to know how you can become a partner in this ministry, write:

The Financial Freedom Foundation, Inc.
P.O. Box 133
Keene, TX 76059
(817) 645-3258

Dr. Hill is available for seminars, workshops, and speaking appointments. For scheduling, call the number above.

Other materials by Dr. Roland J. Hill

The Power of Money—Six powerful presentations on cassette tape on the subject of money.

The *How to Get Out of Debt* workbook—A step-by-step guide to debt reduction.

Wisdom About Wealth—Twelve bound Bible studies about money.

Order from:

The Financial Freedom Foundation, Inc.
P.O. Box 133
Keene, TX 76059
(817) 645-3258

Notes

Chapter One

1. R. C. Sproul, Jr., *Money Matters* (Wheaton, Ill.: Tyndale House Publishers, 1985), 147.

2. Dennis Waitley, *Timing Is Everything* (Nashville, Tenn.: Thomas Nelson Publishing, 1992), 80.

3. Cliff Allbritton, *Dare to Win! How to Live the American Dream* (Nashville, Tenn.: Atlas Crown, 1992), 128.

4. Stephen Covey, *Principle-Centered Leadership* (New York: Fireside Books, 1992), 271, 272.

Chapter Three

1. Paraphrased from Norman Cousins, *In God We Trust* (New York: Harper and Brothers, 1958), 35.

2. Herbert V. Prochnow, *Toastmaster's Quips and Stories* (New York: Sterling Publishing Co., Inc., 1982), 28.

3. Ellen G. White, *Testimonies for the Church, vol. 1* (Mountain View, Calif.: Pacific Press Publishing Association, 1948), 266, 267.

Chapter Four

1. Ellen G. White, *The Ministry of Healing* (Mountain View, Calif.: Pacific Press Publishing Association, 1942), 338.

2. Ibid., 195.

3. Herbert V. Prochnow, *Toastmaster's Quips and Stories* (New York: Sterling Publishing Co., Inc., 1982), 28.

Chapter Five

1. As quoted in Adam Smith, *The Roaring '80s* (New York: Penguin Books, 1990), 269.

2. Ellen G. White, *Christ's Object Lessons* (Washington, D.C.: Review and Herald Publishing Association, 1941), 379.

3. As quoted in Smith, 249.

4. Ellen G. White, *Education* (Mountain View, Calif.: Pacific Press Publishing Association, 1952), 115.

Chapter Six

1. John Murray, *Principles of Conduct* (Grand Rapids, Mich.: Wm. B. Eerdman's Publishing Co., 1981), 82.

2. Ibid., 83.

3. Ellen G. White, *The Cosmic Conflict* (Mountain View, Calif.: Pacific Press Publishing Association, 1950), 438.

4. John Richardson, *Christian Economics* (Houston, Tex.: St. Thomas Press, 1966), 87.

5. Murray, 86.

Chapter Seven

1. Ellen G. White, *Education* (Mountain View, Calif.: Pacific Press Publishing Association, 1952), 17.

2. R.C. Sproul, *In Search of Dignity* (Ventura, Calif.: Regal Books, 1983), 146.

3. Ibid., 148.

Chapter Eight

1. George Fooshee, Jr., *You Can Be Financially Free* (Old Tappan, New Jersey: Fleming H. Revell Company, 1976), 107.

2. Alfred W. Munzert, *Poor Richard's Economic Survival Manual* (Salt Lake City, Utah: Hemisphere Publishing, 1982), 88.

3. Ibid.

4. Peter Wolf, *Land in America: Its Value, Use, and Control* (New York: Pantheon Books, 1981), 27.

5. Ibid., 6.

6. Richard Rice, *The Reign of God* (Berrien Springs, Mich.: Andrews University Press, 1985), 77.

7. Wolf, 24.

Chapter Nine

1. Ellen G. White, *Education* (Mountain View, Calif.: Pacific Press Publishing Association, 1952), 57.

2. Peter Wolf, *Land in America: Its Value, Use, and Control* (New York: Pantheon Books, 1981), 14.

3. Larry Burkett, *The Coming Economic Earthquake* (Chicago, Ill.: Moody Press, 1991), 122, 123.

Chapter Ten

1. Walter E. Wiset, *Health Care and Its Cost – A Challenge for the Church* (Lanham, Maryland: University Press of America, 1988), 168.